Petra R.

Peter K.

Augusta, Gone

A TRUE STORY

Martha Tod Dudman

SIMON & SCHUSTER
New York • London • Toronto • Sydney • Singapore

SIMON & SCHUSTER
Rockefeller Center
1230 Avenue of the Americas
New York, NY 10020

SIMON & SCHUSTER and colophon are registered trademarks
of Simon & Schuster, Inc.

Manufactured in the United States of America

ISBN 0-7432-0409-3

This is a true story,

although some names and details

have been changed.

prologue

MY DAUGHTER LEFT three days ago.

"I'm not telling you where I am," she says when she finally calls. "Don't try to find me."

I don't say anything.

"I'm safe. That's all you need to know," she says.

"I'm glad you called me," I tell her. "When are you coming home?"

"I'm not ever coming home," she tells me.

She hangs up.

She calls back a little before five. I've been crying. I try not to sound like I've been crying, but she can tell.

"Do you want to know where I am?"

"Yes."

"I'm staying with Jude. She's really nice."

"She's Rain's friend?"

"Yeah. She's really nice. She's house-sitting. I'm not telling you where the house is. She has three kitties."

"Can I have the phone number?"

"You can't come get me."

"I'm not going to. I'd like the phone number."

She gives me the phone number.

"I'm not coming home," she tells me.

She calls me every day to tell me she is not coming home. I don't say much. I tell her I miss her. I tell her I love her. I tell her what we had for supper, that we went to the mall and got new socks for Jack, and a belt. I don't tell her about the crying. It feels odd, like being pregnant again, all this crying. How I used to just start crying when certain songs came on the radio. Dumb songs. I'd say, right out loud sometimes, "Oh that's so true!" and then I'd start to cry. So now at odd moments, on my morning walk, driving in the car, when I'm just about to go to sleep, when I'm brushing my teeth, I start to cry. I don't go on and on. I just cry a little. It's like I never get to the real cry that's in me. I just get the top layer. I'm not sure I even want to go down into that inky cavern.

Instead I cry with my mouth open and dragged down at the corners like a tragedy mask. I don't make much noise. I don't want to scare my son, who might hear me and think it's his fault. He misses her too, I remind myself. He doesn't say much about it, but sometimes he asks when she's coming home. I know they talk on the phone when I'm not here.

One day I climb a wet mountain, going up over the old snow and half-melted ice. It's more treacherous, I suppose, in this half-boiled February light and just-above-freezing temperature than in the frantic deep cold of January. The slick of water on top of the ice makes it slippier than when it's just frozen and cold. And the whole trail, really, is ice, like a stream ran down the exact trail and froze there. But I go up anyway. I fall down a few times, but not badly, each time managing to catch myself by grabbing the wet branches of the little trees along the path. Sometimes I go off the trail altogether and crash through dry little bushes and branches along the side, then rejoin the trail farther up. It's not too bad. I've chosen a fairly easy mountain, knowing the steep ones would be too hard and I'd have to turn back. And I really want to get to the top of something. I want to get to the top of this mountain even if there's no view. So I go ahead. I get the back of my pants wet falling down, but I pluck the damp fabric away from my skin and keep going. I make it up and head right back down again. If it were summer, or even if it were sunny, I would stop and sit on a rock and let the sun warm me. As it is the sky is that white gray of February and the colors are all the dark colors of February—the rocks, the leafless trees, the dry bushes—so I just keep going. I think I'll make it all the way up and all the way down and I do.

I want to explain about my walk to my daughter when she calls the third day, but I'm too tired. I keep waking up in the night and thinking that there's something wrong. There *is* something wrong. She's not here. I wake up and I think the phone just rang. And I don't know who called. And then I imagine it was the police and she's in trouble. So I lie awake for a while and I can't get back to sleep and when I do get to sleep I dream strange dreams—the telephone bursts into flames, the door flies open, the sky cracks.

The next day winter break will be over and school will start. She shows up in the middle of the afternoon. I've just gotten back from the grocery store and I'm putting away the food. I got the treats she likes, to lure her back—certain ranch-flavored crackers, almond-poppy muffins, big seedless oranges, watermelon Pop-Tarts, bacon, pink lemonade.

She looks smaller.

"Hi Mom," she tells me.

Then she goes right by me and she goes upstairs.

I hear her go into her room. She comes out again.

"Where's Jack?" she calls down.

"He's at Daddy's," I tell her. "He's spending the night there."

"Oh."

I can hardly hear her. She goes into her room.

I finish putting the groceries away. When I'm done I want to get out of the house. I would like to go for a walk before it gets too dark and too cold, but I think I should say something.

I go upstairs. It's like sticking my hand into the garbage disposal. That's how I feel with her.

She's in her room. She's not listening to music. It's quiet.

I go down the hall and I knock at her door.

"Augusta," I tell her, "I missed you."

"Yeah," she says from in there.

I stand there, in the hall outside her room. I can see a little piece of her floor through the hole where she knocked out one of the boards two years ago when she was really mad. Sometimes I think she's crazy.

"Do you need anything?" I ask her.

"No."

She sounds tired. She's probably exhausted. Probably didn't sleep last night—out all night. Probably didn't eat anything all day. She doesn't like to eat in front of people, so when she's not home she usually doesn't eat.

I wish she could be little again. I would make her Cream

of Wheat and read her stories. Story after story. Whatever she wanted.

"Okay," I tell her. "I'm here."

And I feel as if I've just put my foot on one of those little rocks sticking up out of the ice and I don't know if it's the kind that holds steady or the kind that topples over or the kind that has such a thin layer of ice on top that you can't even see how treacherous it is till you try it.

I

IT WASN'T ALWAYS like this. We used to have wonderful times. There were times when I felt as if I had won two prizes: my two children walking up the road with me. My girl. My boy. Living together in Maine.

There were times when our world seemed perfectly balanced. Later it's easy to remember, when you're mad at yourself and furious with how things came out, to remember only yelling in the kitchen on a winter night and feeling overwhelmed at the office. But I have to remember, too, the happy times when we were all tucked up in bed reading *Mary Poppins* on a winter evening. When we were at the beach with Cynthia and Bea and Sam in summer. When Augusta and I were looking at catalogues together on the green couch while Jack was building buildings in the dining room.

Those things are all true, too.

I raised the kids alone. Their dad and I divorced when they were little, split up when they were two and three and got divorced a year later. When people ask me why we got divorced I say I don't think you have to explain why people get divorced. I think you have to explain how people stay married. How people can stand each other day after day, year after year, rubbing against each other like two bad pennies. But actually I know the exact moment when I decided I had to get away from Ben.

We'd been in Boston at his parents' house for Christmas. We were driving home in the beat-up blue Ford my mother had given us when she got a new one. At least it ran, unlike the rest of the cars that Ben had parked in our driveway to work on when he got around to it. The old green SAAB that just needed some brake work. The red VW that suddenly one day just stopped working.

Of course, the driver's door of the Ford didn't open. You could either slide across from the passenger side or else crawl in through the driver's window. I was starting to mind things like that.

We'd been at his parents' house, which was not like my parents' house. Too many doilies on things. The TV on. Three cats. It was January. It was very cold. We were driving home with both kids in their car seats in the backseat. The car was a mess, full of our junk. Clothes. Blankets. The heat didn't work right so we had the kids bundled up. Juice boxes. Animal crackers. Chewed-on bagels. Christmas wrapping paper. Stuff.

We were coming over the bridge at Bucksport. Ben had to get to work. We were all tired, anxious to get home. He was driving too fast. There was a cop waiting at the Bucksport side and as we slid around the curve he flashed his lights.

"Oh great," Ben said, pulling over opposite the graveyard.

I didn't say anything.

"This is typical," he told me, rolling down his window, letting in the cold hard Bucksport air. "We weren't going any faster than anyone else. They always stop people like us."

That was the moment.

I wasn't people like us. Okies in a beat blue Ford. Full of junk and dirty-faced children. I wasn't like this. I'd grown up in Washington. I was meant for something. My children weren't people like us. If I could have, I would have taken both children, right then, one under each arm, out of that wreck of a car and marched down Route 1 tromp tromp tromp down the highway past the narrow houses up to that flat high place between Bucksport and Ellsworth where you can see so far.

It was a little more complicated than that, but eventually I did leave him. We both stayed in Maine and shared the raising of the children, but most of it fell to me.

I didn't know how I was going to manage. Pay the mortgage. Raise the children. Fix the house. Buy the shoes. And somehow create a life of my own where I would be the star I was meant to be. How all that? I took a job at my mother's radio stations. I worked part-time and then full-time and eventually took over the business. I bought another radio station and found myself going to radio conventions in places like New Orleans and Los Angeles. I always felt as if it were all happening by mistake—the accounting course I took at night so I could read the P&L, the suits and certain shoes I started wearing, learning to use a computer. Suddenly I was worried about ratings and margins and money and negotiating contracts and hiring people and firing people. I was sitting in my office, sitting behind a desk, being a boss, being a businesswoman.

And all this time I was raising my children, coming home at night, changing into soft clothes. Augusta sitting on my bed at night. "I need a private time with you, Mommy." I was fixing supper, washing all the dishes. And sometimes it seemed as if I were doing a wonderful balancing act, balancing it all on the tip of my nose.

Looking back, there were times when I thought I was doing a wonderful job. Being a mother that read to my children, being a mother that talked really talked to my children, finding cool baby-sitters for them like the girl from the College of the Atlantic who practiced Zen and shaved her head and took them to the early-morning ceremony where she became an official Buddhist. Or my dear old friend Marie, who was cozy and sweet and baked them cookies and read them *Narnia* and held them in her lap and loved them. Sometimes I saw my kids on a weekend morning coming in from sledding with their bright bright cheeks and I thought: I am giving them a perfect childhood.

And the time when I took Augusta down to the boat to go out to Great Cranberry Island for a sleepover party and I watched her waiting with her backpack, sitting on a rock by the harbor with her smooth brown hair looking proud and a little worried. And I thought again: I am giving her the perfect childhood. Maine. No locks on the doors. No traffic jams. No vying.

I took them on hikes. I read to them all the time. I told them stories that went on and on. And every spring we went to the circus, each with a friend, all in my car. I left work early and we put on the radio loud and sang along with the oldies. It was early May and always the first warm day of the year, the sky that wonderful tremulous blue of early spring. I was certain my children were having a wonderful life.

It wasn't of course—I was always worried. Worried about money. Worried about being alone forever. Worried about not being a good enough general manager at the radio stations, carrying the tottering pile of my family's fortune, the family business—everything they had was invested in it, my mother told me—on my own shaky incompetent shoulders. I was worried that I had lost hold of who I was, the person I'd defined myself as being—living in Maine, writing stories, walking in the woods—to become a Rotarian, business-woman, firer of employees, wrecker of lives. I was worried I wasn't spending enough time with my children who were so great! though I went to every possible school event, drove them everywhere, went to every performance of every play, every game, everything.

I loved it all—loved the job and resented it. Loved our house and could never keep it nice enough. Loved the children and plucked at them, trying to make them right. How did other people do it?

Oh, I suppose I was in some ways a terrible mother. I yelled. I got impatient. I got mad. I worried over stupid things. I scolded over things that didn't matter. But when I think over the whole long lumpy quilt of my life, the part that makes the most sense, the part that feels the most real and the most dear, is the part where I was cooking in the kitchen and Augusta was coloring at the table and Jack was working on his building. When the house was full of cinnamon and life.

But that's past now. And now we have the scraggly years again. Their scraggle this time. Their struggle. And I am exhausted by it. I feel impatient and deserted. And confused and tired and helpless. And when, after a particularly bitter confrontation, I call my useless log of a boyfriend to shout out my troubles he sighs his heavy sigh like a sofa collapsing and I grow even more impatient. I get so furious. I have to go. I have to grab up my jacket again. I have to storm out of the house. I have to march up the road past the forest past the houses which infuriate me with their lawns. I have to go to the road that turns and heads up Schoolhouse Ledge. I have to walk.

This is how it was and it was nothing like this. There were things that started to happen. But then you don't know. When your daughter is eleven, when your daughter starts to act different, you don't know if it's because her parents are divorced. You don't know if it's because her mother works too much, or because your daughter's too smart for her classes, or because she has maybe a learning disability you never caught, or because her teacher has a learning disability or isn't smart enough to teach your daughter. Or maybe it doesn't have anything to do with school at all. Maybe she is becoming a teenager and this is how they act. Maybe they are supposed to be quiet like this and stay up in their rooms.

And then something happens and you think: I think there's something wrong. I think maybe she's smoking pot. But you don't really believe it because she told you *No Mommy I don't do that, that was somebody else.* And these are the things you think: *Well I smoked pot. But I wasn't only thirteen. I was seventeen when I smoked pot. And it was different then, wasn't it? Wasn't the pot different then? Wasn't it lighter colored? Wasn't it less somehow?* But then you think:

Don't kids do things earlier now? And anyway she said she didn't. And you're not sure and you don't want to not trust her.

I want to trust you, you tell her, looking into her face. I want to trust you when you tell me.

And they say to talk with your children, but she no longer talks to you, and it seems as if it just happened. One day it was just like that. True, she had stopped coming down for breakfast. Stayed up in her room, ran out the door late for school, missed the bus and had to have a ride. But you think, well, that's how they are, aren't they, teenagers? And you try to remember how you were, but you were different and the times were different and it was so long ago. And she's suddenly so angry at you, but then, another time, she's just the same. She's just your little girl. You sit with her and you talk about something, or you go shopping for school clothes and everything seems all right. And you forget how you stood in her room and how the center of your stomach felt so cold. When you found the cigarette. When you found the blue pipe. When you found the little bag she said was aspirin.

And there was that time after eighth-grade graduation when she and her best friend, Alexis, were going to sneak out, but they said they weren't even after you found the cellar door open. But they said they weren't and so you decided to believe them, like that other time when Julie's mother called and told you that Julie and your daughter had stolen some things out of the store downtown and you grounded her and she cried and promised *Never never.* And the time she was supposed to be spending the night at Daisy's but then you found out that her parents didn't know; the girls weren't there. And then there was something and then something else and then you were on a crazy train ride rumbling through a night landscape that you didn't recognize and everything was different and everything normal was gone.

All of a sudden it just happened.

It seems like all of a sudden it just happened.

So now, when I try to remember how it went, it's hard to remember. Augusta was a little girl. Jack was a little boy. I was working too much. There was always too much to do. We were sitting at a table. I was worried about something at work. I got mad about something. I brought my hands down hard on the kitchen table. Augusta cried. Maybe that was it. What made her change.

Whenever it got to be too much for me I would go out. I'd yank my coat off the hook and my mittens off the radiator and head out the door. Just get out and start walking. Up the road big firm steps as if I had somewhere to go. My kids were driving me nuts. This happened all the time now, ever since they started edging into adolescence. They were angry at me. They were scornful. My daughter was furious. My son was bored. I couldn't even remember how it had been anymore; our sweet little household. The candlelit dinners. The fires. The books. The stories and the special treats and the rituals of family I had tended. It had been so long since someone hadn't been mad or exhausted or sad.

ב

I HAVE MY BOYFRIEND but he's sick of me. His children are grown and he lives a quiet, orderly life. When we first started going out it was easy. I had two cute, cuddly children and every other weekend they went off to their father's so we could have romantic every-other-weekend trysts—we went to restaurants, we went to movies, we went away for the weekend to inns. But in the last year or so my children have rarely gone to their father's—or if they do it's in the middle of the week, or just one goes—and though they beg to stay alone in the house I won't let them. Instead I spend the weekend moodily shopping for large amounts of groceries to feed my daughter's bulimia, or wearily cleaning up after them, doing the laundry, going on walks, going on unsatisfying dates with my boyfriend in which we stare glumly at each other across the restaurant table and then go home, he to his house and I to mine because it's suddenly too weird to make love in the house of the children. It's the children's house. They have taken over. So I go for a walk.

If I walk fast, I don't have to think. I can see the lights of the island across the water as I pass the place where the cliff opens out to the sea. The dark rocks far below. The lights are barely visible tonight because the fog's so thick, but I have walked this walk so many times that I know every one of them by heart.

I take the road that goes down to the harbor, where the big fishing boats tied to the pier are ghostly in the yellowy lights of the dock, past the woods, past the stretch of summerhouses, around the cove, and down to what the children and I used to call the Magic Road—a quiet road, used mostly in the summer, that passes between tall trees on either side and then opens out to the harbor. They used to think it was a treat to go that way. Unlike most of the other curvy, hilly roads in town, that road was straight and flat and always perfectly paved. It never had the potholes and frost heaves of the other roads. It was never littered with leaves and branches after a storm in autumn. It was wonderful to bicycle on in summer, and sometimes we imagined that we felt the magic rising out of the road when we went there.

Tonight, going down the road toward the harbor, I walk as if I could walk all night. I think I could. I forget everything when I walk, when I'm into the rhythm of walking, and I could be any one of my selves—in any one of the years that I've lived in this town. I walked before I was married, when I was pregnant with one child, when I was pushing my new baby in her stroller, pregnant with the second. For a time I pushed them both, stuffed into a double stroller. They were so close in age that it was almost as if I had twins. I walked with them when they were little. And later, when they were older, I walked alone again, but sometimes they would still go out with me. My daughter used to walk with me and bring her friends sometimes. We went this way.

The harbor tonight is mysterious and beautiful like a painting. The yellow lights of the dock shine on the boats tied up alongside. The moored boats are just barely visible in the thick fog. The trucks are parked patiently in the lot. The ticket booth is closed for the winter. The harbormaster's building, with its one light lit, is quiet and the harbor's quiet, and the fog is full and thick and it could be another time.

I used to bring the children down here after supper. We'd feed the ducks on summer evenings. The children would race their plastic cars up and down the path and run past tourists, laughing. I'd bring them down after their baths, dressed in their Sleepy LaBeef T-shirts that they used as nightgowns, and they'd climb the big rocks and they'd be so proud.

Then there have been nights like this one, other nights, colder nights, when I came around here looking for my daughter. Driving around looking for my daughter in the night, after calling all of the numbers I've copied down. "No she's not here, can I get your number?" "Give me your number, I'll have her call you." Put away in my little notebook, hidden in the bottom drawer of my desk. Ideas. Numbers. Names. Names of people I've never heard of. Names of people I've never seen. Boys who won't leave their names. Boys who sound like men. Give me your number. Give me your name.

Maybe she's down here, driving around. Late, long after I want to be in bed. Tired from all day at work, but driving around. Dinnertime past. I brought home Chinese food and it sits on the counter in its cartons, getting cold. My son is up in his room—*No, that's all right, I'm not hungry*—waiting. And I'm down here, driving around looking for my daughter.

So many nights like that, and then the nights when I do

find her—barefoot in town, standing near a pay phone with a scrawny boy in a big army jacket and lank blond hair.

"I was just trying to call you," she tells me as she gets into the car. "Can you give Nicky a ride home?"

She calls him Nicky to tell me that he's not a boyfriend. He's too young, too small, too scrawny to be her boyfriend—he's just a kid she knows, someone she takes care of.

It's cold out so I have to let him into the car.

"Where are your shoes?" I ask her.

"Oh I left them somewhere. I had to give them to somebody to wear. Rain was so cold. Anyway, I always go barefoot. You know that."

These are the definitions she has set for herself: she always goes barefoot, she's no good at school, she loves drugs, she smokes, she doesn't like rich people, she's against war, she wears only thrift-store clothes, she doesn't comb her hair.

One by one I release my own rules for my daughter. Rules about when she comes in. Rules about what she wears. Rules about school. Rules about what constitutes sickness. Rules about what constitutes sanity. And each edge she pushes.

Each rule I relinquish brings me closer to some unimaginable abyss. The open chasm. But where it begins, in all this darkness, I can't see. I can only feel my way, feel my way, following her in the darkness. She runs out so quickly and so confidently, calling back lies to me over her shoulder, and I follow her wherever she's going, stumbling along after her in the dark, on the uneven ground where there is gravel, bits of rock, sudden small holes, ice heaves, and somewhere out there, unexpected, without warning, there is a deep vast crater and that's where she's headed. I don't know where it is and I don't know how deep it is and I don't know why she is drawn to it, drawn to it as if in the center of that crater there were a bright light a warmth a magic place that she is drawn to. I can only follow her, rushing along after her voice in the darkness, driving around after her in the darkness, calling to her, catching at her sleeve, at her arm, at her shoulder for a moment, as she hurtles forward. Worrying that I will fall, that I will fall and stumble and fall on the uneven ground, that I will skin my own knees, that she will fall, that I will not catch her in time, will not hold her back, will let her go.

It's been years since I've felt part of the town. When the children were little, before I worked all the time, I used to know people. When we walked downtown for the mail, to get milk, I would see people and I knew their names. At school concerts I knew the other parents, I could talk to them. I knew the teachers. But then, as things got stranger and I got busier, I stopped knowing everyone. My children were in trouble too much. Other parents didn't want my children to play with their children. At first it wasn't like that.

At first it was just a warning, but I didn't get it. One day, two women whom I used to walk with when the children were little stopped me on the street downtown.

"I don't know why you let Jack and Augusta hang out with Ronnie," one of them told me.

"What?" It took me by surprise. I thought we were going to chat.

"I mean it. He's no good. He's trouble. I won't let Jared around him."

I was furious. Ronnie is a big, loping boy with hooded eyes. His mother left, moved out of state. He lives with his father, a lonely man in a wool plaid shirt. One time I was walking by their house and I could hear his father yelling at Ronnie. I could hear Ronnie crying.

"He hasn't had much of a chance, has he?" I asked her now.

"Well, you take the more global view," she retorted. "I guess I'm not that kind. I want to protect my children."

"I think a town like ours can help a boy like Ronnie. I don't think you can give up on a kid when he's fourteen."

"Fifteen," she said as if that's cut it.

I should have paid attention, because a year or two later, people would be warning other parents about *my* children. "I keep them away. I don't let them over. They're no good."

And by then I suppose they were right.

I became busier and busier. Work. Meetings. Off in my car. The only times I went to anything was when I had to. Teacher conferences were no longer the contented exchanges of pleasantries and congratulations they had been when the children were younger. Now I dreaded every phone call from the school. Jack had done something. Been sent out of class. Augusta was in trouble again. She smelled like smoke. She skipped school. She swore in class. She looked stoned. She was missing again. She fell asleep. She said she was sick.

In the car, driving somewhere—to the store, maybe—she starts in on me. "I just want to be free," she tells me. "I need to be free. You can't control me. I want to be my own person. That's my right. You can't control me. Someday I'm just going to go. I'll just leave. You'll see."

I want to think it's just drugs. She's taking drugs. I know that. She is taking all kinds of drugs. I find marijuana in her room. I know it's not the gentle grass of the sixties. They treat it with something now, don't they? It's powerful. I remember the last time I smoked, years ago. And there are pills. I find big messy capsules full of beige powder on the floor of her room. I find what I think is probably blotter acid. I find little white pills. What are they? I don't know.

So I tell myself it's drugs. She's stoned a lot of the time. Either she's getting high or else she's coming down off something. But I'm afraid it's something else. I'm afraid it's more than that. I'm afraid of her.

When I cleaned her room, I found old packages of cookies. She'd lied about these just as adamantly as about the drugs. "No, I didn't eat them. Ronnie did. He came over one night and took a package." Her lies were clumsy and inaccurate, but I allowed them. I didn't want her to think I doubted her. Why not? I didn't want to have her look at me that way and say, "You never believe me! You always think I'm lying! You don't trust me!"

By this time she was not going to school. She stayed only sometimes at the house. She crashed with friends or said she did. She went to parties and returned days later, barefoot, dirty, saying she had to sleep, and then would sleep all day and wake sad and hungry and furious with me.

Where was I all that time? I was there. I was trying to make sense of it. I was still trying to put it into a box it might fit neatly.

I didn't know if it was adolescent behavior or craziness or my fault or all three. It happened so quickly. So quickly she went from being a somewhat difficult, kind of moody girl to what she finally became, which made me feel crazy.

There were nights when I took a flashlight and walked around the town up this same road through the same dark, looking for her.

There were nights when I drove around to every place that maybe kids might go, looking for her.

There were the phone calls I made, "I'm sorry, I know it's late, but have you seen my daughter?"

And there were the odd, strained conversations with the other parents, when we would commiserate, "Oh it's hard, I know, teenagers!" rolling our eyes, sitting on the chilly metal bleachers at the baseball game. We exchanged complaints the way we used to exchange photographs of our babies.

"You should see her room!"

"I know! and every night the same old fight about homework!"

And I'm thinking: Homework? That was long gone, the idea of homework.

The last time I went to a game we went over the usual: eating disorders, worries about drugs, staying out late, driving, drinking and driving. I didn't dare introduce the next tier: stealing, staying out all night, hitchhiking to Boston, screaming at the top of her lungs, holding up a knife one time, holding it up and looking at me, telling me what she would like to do with it—my daughter! my daughter! my girl.

I stayed away after that, from the games, from the other mothers with their smug problems and their rolling eyes.

It's as if I have a disease and none of them want to catch it. My daughter has a disease. My family is disintegrating, and though they don't say it I know what they are thinking— she got divorced, she didn't go to church, she wasn't on the PTO, she worked too much. All my sins corroborated by the terrible fix I'm in. I know what they tell one another in their kitchens, where they take cookies out of ovens that are always clean, where their families eat together at the table, father mother sister brother—not like at our house, where Jack sits and eats with forced heartiness while Augusta sits and glares at me until I let her go.

One time in the middle of everything I was driving home from work listening to *All Things Considered,* and there was a story about a young boy somewhere in America who had died playing baseball in Little League. And they said he had died because he had been hit in the chest with a ball. And they did a little story about how a number of kids die every year from getting hit in the chest with a ball, which is why the catchers wear chest pads. Because the chests of children are still soft, the bones still flexible, the force of the blow, if it's hard enough, can push the bones inward. If the ball hits the chest of the child in a certain way, at a certain angle, when the heart is expanded to a certain degree, it just kills him.

I want to say how we went from being the three of us in the house eating supper at the table into the dark whirling storm of the next few years, but even now, looking back, I don't know what happened. There wasn't any one thing. There wasn't any map to follow, certain roads I see now I should have avoided. It was the divorce. It was my working. It was my anger. It was their father. It was me. It was living in Maine. It was the school. It was genetic. It was a baseball—flung out through the late sun of the afternoon, angled just right, flying through the air—that hit my daughter.

3

ONE MORNING, just as I am leaving for work, I get a call from my daughter.

"I don't feel good," she tells me in her sick voice. "I can't be here. But they won't let me leave. I need you. I want to go home."

I tell her to wait for me at school. She's playing me, but I am stupidly, gamely, predictably thrilled that she called me. It's like the other little shabby bits that I dredge up out of our sad and futile relationship: proof that she loves me, that she needs me.

"I'll be right there," I tell her in my mommy voice.

I call the office, tell them I'll be late. They're used to this by now. I'm often late. My life's a crisis that they don't quite comprehend. They don't know all the figures on the landscape, but they know what the landscape looks like—it's been bombed. I imagine them, all of them, at their desks, exchanging glances. They are broadcasters reporting on distant wars. "She's going to be late," they tell one another.

"Another shelling." I have been humbled. I am stumbling through the rubble. Work's just incidental to my life.

I drive over to the high school, park the car, walk into the building. Augusta's sitting on the floor in the hallway, leaning up against the wall next to her friend Rain. They're both wearing overalls. Rain had her head shaved. Her nose is pierced. Augusta wants her lip pierced. Rain's got her navel pierced. Augusta wants her eyebrow pierced.

"Hi, Martha," Augusta says sarcastically.

"Hi."

I stand in front of them, looking down. Augusta's wearing Birks. Rain is wearing what we used to call engineer boots. They're both such pretty girls.

"What's going on?"

"I have to go home."

"Are you sick?"

"Nursie says I'm not sick. Nursie said I had to call you. I can't take this. Psychically I can't take it."

"Have you got a fever?"

"I don't have a fever."

"Are you going to throw up?"

"I'm not bulimic."

"I think you need to stay in school."

"But Martha!"

"You don't understand, Martha," Rain tells me seriously. "This place is bad for us. They're so fucking dumb here. They don't get it."

"A lot of things are dumb," I tell them. "You just have to get through it."

"I can't, Mommy!"

"You have to. This is what you have to do right now. Go to school. Get through it. Then you get to pick."

"But I don't feel good."

"Do you think I feel good? Do you think I love going into work every day? You just do it. You do it because that's what you do."

"Why don't you just quit then?"

"Because your father doesn't give me any fucking child support."

The minute I say it, I can't believe I've said it. I've never said it. I've never admitted it before. I've always been oblique, even though I know she knows. But now I've not only said it, I said it with "fucking." Two more things to feel guilty about. But I'm rabid. I'm sick of all this—everything not going right. Phone calls from the school. Phone calls from Augusta. Everything always off-kilter.

"Just go to school," I tell her finally.

"No," she says.

I want to yell but I've quit yelling. I stand there in my work suit furious and hopeless. I hated school too. I know what she means. The dead hallway. The inevitable classes. I always hated it. The teachers droning on and on about stuff that doesn't matter, that is separate from life. The windows. The floors. The desks. I hated school. I probably taught them to hate school; passed it along like a blight.

"Fine," I say instead of ranting. And I go out.

Halfway to the car I realize I can't just leave. I turn and go back into the school, but they're gone.

I go down to Bill's office. He's the vice principal and an old friend by now. It's his job to call the parents of the children who go astray. We're well acquainted.

"I don't know what to do with her," I tell him.

He rolls his eyes.

"I'm so sick of this."

"You and me both," he tells me.

He gestures toward his telephone. "Just got a call from Smoky. Two girls, name of Augusta and Rain, just seen headed for the far field."

"What are they doing?"

"Just walking there. So far, just walking out there."

The phone rings. He picks it up, his eyes on me. Speaks into the phone. "Yeah. Right. Okay. Nah. I got the mother here. She'll go after them."

He hangs up the phone.

"They're headed down the road," he tells me.

I sigh and run out, down the hall, past a couple of kids going from one class to another. Run across the parking lot. And it just registers, as I run toward my car, how blue the sky is today, how warm the early spring sun, what a beautiful day it's turning out to be.

But I go the wrong way. Either they've already been picked up, or they've gone into the woods, or they went the other way. I drive futilely up and down a few times. No one. Finally, knowing they're gone, I head for home. Maybe they'll come here. I think of hiding the car and waiting in the house, just in case, but they're too shrewd for that. So I just go in, heavily, and call my office.

"Anything going on?"

There are a couple of messages for me. But nothing I have to do right this minute.

I call the school. "Anything?"

I can imagine Bill smiling his grim smile. "Nothing here. Any luck?"

"No. I drove up and down but I didn't see them. You call Rain's mother?"

"Sure."

"Okay. Well, let me know if you hear anything."

33

"Will do."

"I guess I'll be at the office."

I think I ought to eat something, but food, like so much of my life these days, seems like an odd chore, disconnected to anything else—hunger, desire. I take something, a bagel, an apple, a piece of cheese, in case I can stand to eat it later. I leave the house and go out down our plain steps into our plain yard, and again I am struck by the beauty of the day. I can smell spring, even though it's not quite here yet. The sun feels warm on my shoulders. I'm still wearing my work clothes, but I'd love to rip them off, pull on a pair of old jeans and a T-shirt, feel the air on my skin for the first time in months! Feel the air on my winter arms, turn my winter face to the sun. I'd like it if I didn't have anything to do this afternoon. No work. No looking for lost daughters. No obligations.

For a few minutes I stand in my shabby yard in front of my house and allow myself to imagine a day without duties. A day without phone calls and hurry. I'd let my shoulders slump. They always seem up around my ears these days, hunched for the next hit. I'd go for a walk, but a different kind of a walk—not the kind where you hurry because you've only got half an hour and then have to be back to do something else, but a long walk, an ambling kind of a walk. A walk not for exercise (eat food, walk body) but a walk for the joy of it. An amble. A ramble. A meandering through the town, through the woods. I would taste the air of springtime. I would let my thoughts roam.

But it's time to go.

I hop into my car. The sun shines through the sunroof and I love the feel of it. I back out of the driveway fast and I snap the wheel around and plunge out onto the road. As I'm passing a big stretch of woods on my way up 198, I see Rain's mother, Jenny, heading toward me in her determined little blue-black Volvo. I stick my arm out the window, wave at her, and from inside her car she waves back. I pull over. She swoops around, pulls in behind me, gets into my car.

There's no preamble. We hardly know each other.

"Any ideas?"

"None."

Rain, it turns out, has been missing for four days.

"She always has to tell me where she is. That's my only rule," Jenny tells me. "But she called and told me she was going to take off for a concert in Boston with Jude. I told her I thought it was fine that she wanted to go to the concert, but that this wasn't the time for it. That she had work to do. That she had to go to school now. But she went anyway. The first I heard she was back was when Bill called to tell me she'd left again with Augusta."

"Where do you think they went?"

"God knows. They'll go anywhere. But not far, they don't have any money. Probably they're at somebody's house now. One of their loser friends."

"Getting high."

"Yeah, maybe."

Jenny looks away. I guess she doesn't think it's so bad for kids to get high.

"I've decided I'm going to take her to her father's."

"Really?"

"I can't take it anymore. It's too hard on Phoebe. It's too hard on me. It's gotten too crazy. She's stoned all the time. She's stealing from me. We had this money we were saving in a little china jar in the kitchen. You know, putting spare change in. We were going to buy bicycles with it. For all of us. And I went in one day and all the money was gone. And I just went into her room and I held up the jar and I looked at her. And she didn't even apologize. All she said was, 'I just borrowed it. I was going to put it back.'"

Jenny is so gentle and pretty. She's younger than I am. We were in birth class together a long time ago. She wears tons of rings and long skirts and works in an office answering the phones.

She's divorced, too, but she lives with someone.

So now she's thinking about sending Rain to her father's. That's what some of us do. When it gets too rough. When it gets too crazy. I've thought about it myself. Sending Augusta to her father's.

We talk about the girls as if they were soldiers apart from us.

And while we're talking there in the car I see them coming out of the woods just up ahead.

I put my hand out. "Wait," I whisper. "I see them."

"Where?"

"There—right there, up ahead. Is Rain wearing a blue backpack?"

"She's got one."

We're whispering. As if the car itself were invisible, like if we're very quiet they won't know we're there.

"Come on."

Together, as quietly as we can, we open our doors, and we go quietly into the forest, but just as we get out of the car they see us, and they turn and disappear into the trees.

We go after them, but we don't know which way to go. We stand calling, yelling into the sunny woods. They're gone. Jenny goes bravely up the trail in her long skirt. She is wearing maybe a dozen silver bracelets on her wrist, and they make a merry sound and catch the light as it shines through the trees. I feel large and ungainly coming along behind her

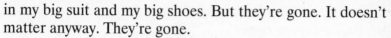

in my big suit and my big shoes. But they're gone. It doesn't matter anyway. They're gone.

We stand together in the sunny woods.

"Nice day for a hike," Jenny says ruefully.

I feel like we're best friends now.

At the car we hug each other. Because it's daytime it feels like an adventure, not a nightmare. They're missing, but the sun is out. We've seen them and the woods are cheerful.

"Augusta knows her way through the woods," I tell Jenny, hoping it's true. "Call me if you hear anything."

We exchange all our numbers.

And I drive off to work.

One minute I'm standing in the woods, then all of a sudden I'm sitting at my desk. It's funny, working during a crisis. It frees you, somewhat, from taking anything too seriously. I'm actually running the company better than when I was all on top of it with all my anxieties and pickiness. It's a good machine and it chugs ahead. People come to me with their problems and worries and they seem so tiny that I can fix them easily. They're a relief. A relief from my life, which is so unwieldy and so crazy right now.

It's still light when I leave work. Late March. The days feel so luxuriously long after the short, brutal days of real winter. I'm buoyed up by my busyness. I turn on the radio and listen to the *Oldies Request Hour* on Magic 95.7 with the Humble but Nonetheless Mighty John. Somebody calls in a request for "Chapel of Love," which Augusta and I used to sing along to in perfect, pristine a cappella—the only song we ever got quite right.

At home there's a note from Jack. He's got practice, he won't be home until later.

A message on the machine from Jenny. "Martha. Call me."

We talk in secret code to hinder speculation by the enemy.

I call her up and she tells me she has a number. She thinks she knows where they might be. "That little house, the one with all the junk in the yard, just up on 198 near the Old Schoolhouse?"

I know the one. "Do you want to go there?"

"I can't leave Phoebe."

"I'm going up. I'll call you when I find them."

I feel strong and powerful and tall. I call my ex. He tells me he'll be down.

Together we drive over to the shabby cottage by the side of the road. I'd been there once before. One New Year's Eve Augusta told me she was going to a party there. On a hunch, a whim, a something of uncertainty, I went there, "Just to see," I told myself. "Just to see."

It was bitter cold when I rapped on the screen door that night. A short girl with big breasts and dyed blond hair and black black eye makeup answered the door.

"I'm looking for Augusta," I told her.

She smiled at me. The house behind her smelled of grass and cigarette smoke.

"I want to give her my telephone number where I'll be," I invented.

She smiled and let me in.

We stood in a little kitchen with too low a ceiling. There was a little table with an overflowing ashtray and some dirty glasses. A stove. A short refrigerator. A dirty braided rug. Around the whole wall all the way around the room, about chest high, was a little shelf, and on the shelf, in a neat row a line of brown beer bottles, empties.

"She isn't here," said Blondie.

"She told me she was coming here," I said.

"She was here, but she left. They went to get somebody. Her and Kyle."

Ah, Kyle!

"Well, I just wanted to give her my number. Where I'll be."

She looks at me. We're still standing in the kitchen, but I can see into the next room. It's a small room, like the innards of a trailer, with a sagging brown plaid couch and something dark hung over the window. There's a cheap fake-wood coffee table covered with ashtrays and half-empty glasses and beer bottles and Pepsi cans. I know that there are cigarette butts floating in the Pepsi cans. I sense it. A boy about nineteen with big pants is sprawled out on the couch. He looks balefully out at me through the kitchen doorway.

"Do you have a pen?" I ask her.

This is a tough one for Blondie. A pen. But she is up to the challenge. "Will a pencil do?" she asks me like a busy secretary.

"Sure."

She gets me one. It's barely sharpened. Someone has been busy with their geometry in this house!

I write the number down. I hand it to her.

"Tell her I'll call later," I warn her, like she cares.

"Okay."

The boy continues to stare at me from the brown plaid couch until I leave.

Where is the music? I wonder. It's New Year's Eve.

✿

This time a lank boy, different boy, comes to the door. He opens just the big door, but the dog butts past him and comes out and barks at us too close.

The screen slaps shut, the boy's behind it.

"I came to get my daughter."

"What's her name?"

"Augusta."

"She's not here."

"I know she's here."

"Just a minute."

He pulls the dog inside, goes in, is gone awhile.

"How do you know she's here?" Ben asks me.

"She's here, don't worry," I tell him.

Ben goes around to the side of the house, tries looking in the window, but I could have told him the windows all have dark cloth hung on the inside. He won't be able to see in.

The lank boy comes back. This time he is holding the dog in his arms.

"They're not here," he tells me.

"I want to see them."

"They don't want to see you," he tells me.

"I don't care. You've got my daughter in there. She's fifteen. I'm coming in," I tell him and I open the door and brush right past him. Ben stands behind me, uselessly. I go into the same house. Except for the outside temperature, it's just like New Year's Eve. No blond girl, but plenty of beer bottles.

"Hey!" the boy says from behind me. "You can't just come into my house!"

I don't even bother to answer. I am clenched inside. I go right through the despairing little kitchen with its pitiful cruddy little row of beer bottles, its sad counter, right through the depressing living room into another room. Mat-

tress on the floor. Nobody around. Old clothes all over.
Small television set with broken antenna on the same coffee
table. I call to her, "Augusta?"

Then back through the living room, in through the
kitchen, where the boy still stands with his dog in his arms
like a big hairy useless angular child, I walk right past him to
the other bedroom. This one's worse. I can smell the deceit.
I can smell the sad torn sex of the place, the dirty laundry of
the place, the yeast-infections, old-beer, cigarette-butt smell
of the place. The stale pennies, the crumpled dollar bills, the
old-pizza, faded-baseball smell of a place like this.

There's a shallow closet with a curtain hung over it. I can't
believe it. They still use those same damn Indian bed-
spreads.

There, wedged into the narrow space, my two girls
squeezed in together. My daughter staring up at me with big
stoned acid-crazed eyes.

"Hello, Augusta," I say calmly. "Hello, Rain."

"Hi, Mommy."

"Let's go."

"I'm not going without Rain."

"I'm not going."

"Let's go," I tell them pleasantly, while in my mind I'm
skittering with possibilities: what if they don't come? then
what? what do I—yank them out? The dog starts barking?
The lank boy coming after me? Police?

But then, amazingly, they do come with me, out into the
gentle new spring evening, into the car.

"We need to talk," I tell them.

"Where are we going?" Rain asks suspiciously as I take
the turn toward her town, down the road.

"We need to talk," I say and flip the little flip that locks
the doors in back, for child safety.

41

It makes them go crazy, yelling, and in the front seat Ben argues with them. What are they even yelling about? I think they might be arguing about politics, Buddhism, one of those stoned savage conversations I remember. Rain meanwhile kicking at my seat. Augusta yelling, "You can't kidnap us!"

Ben trying, in his kind and futile way, to have a conversation. Me thinking fine, I don't care what you talk about, just talk, just argue, just remain oblivious as we get closer to Rain's house.

I have no plan. I'm thinking somehow if we separate them, get Rain to Jenny, then the two of us can surely handle one furious short fifteen-year-old high on something— what? What do they take these days? Horse tranquilizers? LSD? Crank, crack, smack, speed? Do they take anything as we took anything? Look! It's organic! Brown dusty powder in a dusty cap.

Ah, Augusta! Don't you think I understand the pull? The pull of the inexpressible cosmic wonder? The pull of the final belonging? The pull of the rim of the world, where to wander is as enchanted as the magic books I used to read you when we snuggled up together in my bed? We're made one way, my daughter, you and I. And where the others walk, we like to fly.

4

I HAVE NO PLAN. We pull into the long drive to the little house where Jenny lives with Rain and Phoebe. Suddenly I lay my hand down flat on the horn and let it rip out into the gathering night. Headlights on! Shine at the house! Horn blasting! The girls tumble out of the backseat, fling themselves out of the car, start running back down the driveway.

We go after them and behind us the door opens and Jenny in her swaying long skirt comes out. "What is it?"

"We've got them!" I yell back over my shoulder as I run down the driveway, hoping this once that Ben will do something. And he does. He grabs Augusta as I run after Rain, who shakes me off. I grab her. She shakes again at me, she tries to hit me, but she's really just a kind nice girl who likes me. I have made her sandwiches. She doesn't want to hit me. She tries to shake me off, tosses her head up in her little way. I hang on. Ben is yelling. *I can't hold her, Martha!* So I lurch back, dragging Rain. Phoebe is sitting on the steps staring at us. There's confusion, yelling, fighting. Augusta, kicking out, kicks Ben.

Kicks me. We drag her and stuff her back into the backseat. Ben holds her down, and as we back off down the drive I see Rain lying on the ground with Jenny on her, holding her down. It's as if our girls were wild criminals. As if we were the cops.

Augusta in the backseat yells and flails and punches at me with her hands.

"I'm trying to drive!" I yell back.

(Augusta in her car seat yelling, fed up with the endless ferrying around, being taken here and there, wanting to be in charge. *It's my body!* she used to tell me, tells me still.)

"Ben! Hold her!"

"I'm trying to!"

We reach across the abyss of our long divorce, reach back to each other.

He turns around in the seat, grabs her, holds her arms so she can't punch me. She twists her head around, she tries to bite him, drums with her feet, kicks at the seat.

"You stop it!" he says, finally. "Just cut it out."

The drive is endless.

I wonder about putting on the radio.

What the hell do we do now?

We head back to the house. Open the car doors, haul her out, pull her into the house. For what?

For hours and hours of a grisly scene. Much of it spent in the kitchen with the lights blaring and glaring and Jack standing in the doorway alarmed and furious, but not sure why or at whom, mad at all of us, made crazy by the fighting and the yelling. Augusta yelling. Screaming at me how she'd like to kill me. How she'd like to take a knife and stab me. How she hates me. How she hates Daddy. How she just wants a life (starts crying), wants some freedom. Why don't we let her go? Why don't we let her be free? That's all she wants. Is freedom. That this is her one life. That this is her only one life. She is crying furiously, throws things at us, and yells and yells and yells.

And I am silenced, finally, silenced by her yelling. There are no answers to her cries and shouts. I can't reply. She can't hear anything I say.

Is this how she felt when I used to get so mad (so mad, she'd tell me) when she was a little girl? That there are no possible doors out? That I would rant and rant and that my ranting was somehow opaque, that I couldn't hear her even if she thought of some clever way to wedge into my ranting?

Oh, I don't know. I am exhausted.

Jack is in the doorway and I can feel him quivering. I can feel his rage. I can feel his uneasiness boiling up, boiling up. It's a hot awareness like, I think, being peeled, and being forced, as he's forced now, to take in all these diverse and disturbing things at once: His father, who doesn't live here, in the kitchen. His mother furious and frightened. And his sister screaming and screeching. It's too late. He hasn't eaten. Isn't it time for dinner now? Isn't it time to have the dinner now? The phone rings! Yelling! Everyone is crazy and he's crazy too and suddenly, when someone glances aside, Jack leaps forth, grabs Ben right around the throat with his strong arm, and chokes him, chokes him. Hard.

And Ben is red faced, choking, coughing, trying to pull him off, but Jack won't get off. He is *on* now. He is strong!

"Stop it, Jack!" I tell him like a dog.

He stops, steps back.

"I can't stand this!" he yells at all of us: at the kitchen with its too-bright lights; at his sister with her yelling; at me, his mother crazy in the night; his father, who does not belong here: all of us making him do this, all of us making him nuts.

We disperse then. Augusta goes upstairs.

"I'm packing," she tells us. "Don't think I'm giving up."

I think she's gone up there to smoke a cigarette.

She turns the music on real loud and slams her door.

Jack wobbles off. "I'm going out," he tells me.

"You okay?" I ask my ex.

"Yeah."

Ben rubs his neck. "He really hurt me. He was really choking me. He had me there."

"Are you okay?"

I'm shivering. I don't know what to do. This is my family.

Later, Ben and I sit in the living room. I've called the teen emergency suicide-prevention hot line in the phone book. I've been told that my daughter is "in an oppositional phase" but since I don't (really) feel she is an immediate danger to me or to herself, they can't help me. They offer some dull advice about family counseling. Okay, sure, but how do we get through the next twenty minutes?

We do, of course. We are like raggedy survivors in the living room. Jack comes back in. We talk in quiet voices. Finally, Augusta comes downstairs.

I go into the kitchen, come out with a box of crackers, eat a couple, hold it out to her. I know she's really hungry. She takes the box with resignation, eats a few. I go get her some juice. Cranberry. The kind she likes.

"But I still want freedom," she reminds us. "One of these days I'm just going to take off. And you'll never find me."

This is not, I think, going on in everybody's house. This is not going on behind the tall trees of the Havilands' house.

This is not happening at the homes with two parents. This is not happening at the homes where the mother doesn't work. So it is my fault. I'm divorced. I work too much. I don't go to church. I'm too erratic. It's Ben's fault. He doesn't do things right. He isn't around enough. He's too erratic.

What I thought was our strength and our originality, our quirkiness, what made us special, is finally our downfall. We're lousy parents and now we have lousy kids.

Later, after we sent her away, I would miss her so much, so much. But when I was honest with myself, I knew that I didn't want to go back to that. No matter how much I missed her. I couldn't go back to that time of emergency and crisis after crisis. Back to the flashing lights. Back to the perilous lull that came after a scene like that, when we all went off into our own rooms, went to bed.

The next morning we were up as usual, taking our ritual turns in the bathroom, kids coming down late to school, narrowly making the bus, grabbing their lunches on the way out. I still made their lunches every morning, as if they would actually eat them. As if they would find the special cookies, the sandwiches, the little bags of chips, and know their mother loved them. Afterward, when Augusta was gone and the school opened up her locker, we found dozens of squashed lunch bags with the rotting lunches inside. Sandwiches pressed down, the apples mushy. I suspected that she never ate them, but whenever I asked her, she would always say, "No, you have to make my lunch, Mommy! You have to!"

5

I USED TO have friends. Plenty of friends. I had friends for different occasions. Friends I took walks with. Friends who had kids my kids' age. Friends who were men who might become lovers. Friends who were men who used to be lovers. Friends I had known forever. Friends I never really liked that well. Friends I truly loved. Friends that were good for being silly with. Girlfriends. Friends who were smarter than I was. Friends who read a lot. Friends who lived the kinds of lives I might have lived. Friends from childhood. Friends from high school. Friends from college. Friends I met by accident.

But I hadn't seen them lately. Because when my life started to fly apart my friends, all of them, scratched against my skin like uncomfortable sweaters. Anything they said was the wrong thing. When Susan said to me, "How's Augusta doing?" I wanted to kill her. When my friend Lydia called from Washington to tell me about her daughter's triumph onstage, her summer in France with a roving theater group, I felt as if she were torturing me on purpose. I didn't want to show anyone my ruined face.

So I burrowed in. I burrowed away from the light and the others. I kept to myself. I had plenty to do, certainly. I was so busy. Busy with the radio stations. Busy with the house. Busy, as I told someone if they called, busy with the children. I had to pick them up. I had to drive them somewhere. I had to pick Augusta up at jazz band. She might need a ride to driver's ed. She might be wandering barefoot through town at 4 A.M. and I might need to go look for her. She might be yelling at me all morning and I wouldn't be able to speak. She might be so stoned that I had to stay downstairs, pretending to do something in the kitchen so I could stop her if she tried to go out the door.

So I was busy pretty much all the time. And the friends with their own stupid problems and their aspirations seemed so petty. What did I care if Howard had had an argument with his brother? I was alone with the struggle. If anything, their occasional sympathy was worse. It was better to be by myself. Sooner or later I'd figure out how to fix things, find the right thing to say, the magic charm.

Easter 1998. I decided we would have a nice family dinner. We had always had dinner with my parents, but there was no way we could all get ourselves in the car and drive two hours to be with them. I never made plans anymore except for the odd, broken, skeletal structure of my work hours, the children's school. But Easter. I would roast a chicken. I would make Easter baskets. I would have mashed potatoes. I would have salad, little peas. A pie.

It was, amazingly, a beautiful day. The long, straggly, cold, gray end of winter seems to last forever in Maine, but once in a while there are little bright pockets of perfect soft spring days. That Easter Sunday was a sunny gift.

The children slept until noon. When they came downstairs, I was already up and making the pie. Augusta seemed content. She peeled some apples for me at the kitchen table. Jack went off with friends. I took my walk.

In the late afternoon, when I came in to finish making supper, set the table, light the candles, something in the house had changed.

Augusta was in her room, but something had changed.

Jack was on the phone, but something had changed.

I called them down. Augusta came into the kitchen.

"I don't want to eat."

Her face was set. "I don't feel good. I don't think I want anything to eat."

"I made it," I said simply, to guilt her into it.

Jack skips down. He's starving. "Roast chicken!" he says delightedly, then right away reads the room.

Sees the way Augusta is, in her implacable little way, slowly doing it again—sucking the air out. Sucking all the air out of the room, until nobody but Augusta can breathe.

Sees my edginess moving toward fury.

Sees my despair.

Reads his own sad role (again!) as arbiter, as placater, as lone man, kind man, priest in this house of hormones.

"Let's eat!" he tells us. He's too young for this. Anyone would be too young for this.

But somehow it works. She'll still sit down for him. We have the meal.

The food's like big things made of rubber in our mouths. Made of rug fluff. Made of shit.

Augusta gobbles down a drumstick, shoves at her potatoes, sips her milk.

"This is disgusting," she says in a mean voice.

"Can't you eat? It's Easter," I tell her, like that might fix
it.

But of course Easter is the reason. The holidays are particular targets for her. Of course. Let's wreck the holidays!
These most of all! These shiny baubles. These china fig-
urines. The little shepherd girl in her blue china skirt and
puffy sleeves. The golden princess with gilt ribbons and a
painted china crown. The cunning piggy. Smash them.
Smash them all.

She looks at me in her baleful, hateful way, "So? I'm a
Buddhist. I don't celebrate Easter. And you're a Jew."

"I know. I celebrate it purely as a commercial holiday,"
I say, "like Christmas," trying to play that old sardonic
game we used to play, we atheists together, we the chosen.
But I haven't got the spirit for it now. I'm much too tired.
I'm too sad, too wounded, too disgusting—plate full of
food that I don't even want. (Jack, clattering along with false
heartiness, asks for a second helping of potato and says
without saying, "This is good, Mommy, this is great. Isn't this
fun?")

"May I please be excused?"

We've been here seven minutes. Maybe.

"Can't you wait?"

"What for?"

"This is Easter. This is a family meal. This is what makes
us a family."

"We're not a family. You're hardly like a mother. Fine. I'll
wait. How long?"

"I don't know, Augusta. Could you just sit there? Could
we just talk? I made this dinner."

"Stop it!" Jack says.

Augusta puts her napkin on her food and turns her chair a little so it faces mine.

"This isn't a family. Families are stupid, anyway. You don't choose your family. You get stuck with them. When I grow up I'm not having a family. I'm just going to live with people I care about. I'll have cats. You think you can turn us into a family by making us have a meal together? It's not going to work. We aren't a family. There's no such thing as families, especially if they're forced on you. I can't wait to grow up and get away from you. The minute I'm eighteen—"

"Okay," I tell her wearily. "Go ahead. Just leave."

I sit in silence at the table when she's gone. I can't help myself. I know I have to brighten up for Jack, but I can't do it.

He's miserable. Now he's stuck sitting here with his mouth full of food.

The pie's ready.

"You want some?" I ask him, taking it out of the oven. It smells delicious. It's apple pie. His favorite.

"I'm pretty full," he tells me. "Maybe later. I think I'll go shoot some baskets. Is that okay?"

"Sure," I tell him. This is horrible.

I get up, and eleven minutes after we sat down I am scraping the plates into the trash can. Doing the dishes. As I stand at the sink, doing the dishes alone in our kitchen, I can see Jack out in the driveway shooting basket after basket. Making every one of them. I can hear Augusta up in her room listening to music very loud.

I do the dishes and I cry. I hate myself.

❧

Four days later the chicken's still in the refrigerator. I've been planning soup. I think I'll make it one night after work. It doesn't take long. I could make it—a nice chicken soup with rice in it. But on the fifth day I can't stand seeing it anymore. I throw it out. And when I hear the carcass of the Easter chicken fall into the garbage with a heavy thump, I think maybe that will fix everything.

I go back to see the woman in Bangor. My daughter saw her one time. She's a psychologist. Someone recommended her as pretty hip. Maybe good for Augusta, who agreed to go once and actually seemed to like her, but refused to go again.

"I don't like her *that* much," she told me.

We sat together on the lady's beige couch. I liked the office. Nice odd art, and the woman was big and had good jewelry and a long skirt. Something I might wear. I liked her.

"I'll be happy to see Augusta when she's ready to do some work," the woman told me. "She doesn't really seem prepared to do that yet, and frankly, without that desire, nothing's going to happen."

On the drive home Augusta was triumphant.

"I told you that it wouldn't work," she said. "I'm never going back."

But now I think *I'll* go back.

"I don't know what to do," I tell the woman.

This is mostly what happens when I see her. I tell her I don't know what to do.

It was amazing how fast it got worse. I don't remember the sequence really anymore. It was always, I know now, worse than I thought.

I wanted her to quit smoking.

That seemed pretty important for a while.

Then I was still struggling with the pot when she was deep into acid.

I was still worried about the disappearing cookies—bags of them! whole packages of chips! candy wrappers!—when she was starving herself.

I was still wondering how she was going to pass Spanish when she had stopped, really stopped, going to school.

And all the while, through all of it, the drumbeat of my failure. On my walks, my failure. At night, sleepless, my failure. The divorce, my failure. The things I said or didn't say. The times I yelled too much or yelled too little. Money. Things I bought or didn't buy. Times I should have. Times if only I'd. All of it lost! Lost! Lost in the spin.

Then there were all the carefully tailored stories for the people I still spoke with. As for the other parents—forget them! They were in another pasture altogether. They were in another town. They were on another, better planet. But I still had my parents.

"How's she doing?" they'd ask me seriously, sadly. My mother itching to tell me how terrible I'd been. Enough with *your* problems! Let me tell you about *you!* How *you* were! How we struggled! How we suffered! The things *you* did! The time *you!* How *you!* Okay okay okay.

"How's she doing?"

I know they are still thinking of the night I asked them to supper and Augusta wouldn't come down. She stayed in her room with the lights off and the dark curtains drawn.

"Your grandparents are here," I told her in that pleading,

placating tone. I hate myself, I hate hearing myself say it, but I say it anyway. "Remember? I told you they were coming to supper. Can you come down?"

"I can't," she groans. "I can't. I feel sick."

"Well, you don't have to eat. Just come down."

"I can't!"

"They want to see you."

"All right. All right. Just leave me alone."

Later she does stagger down the stairs. She looks terrible. She's wearing her worst clothes. Old ratty too-big jeans. A brown sweatshirt with a stain down the front and ripped-out neck. She's barefoot. Her hair's uncombed and hanging down her face. She goes into the living room, says wanly, "Hi Grandma. Hi Grandpa."

I go into the kitchen. Start getting out the food.

I hear their voices. They are talking to her. I can't hear her answer, but I think maybe they are telling her something. My father telling her some jokes. Jack's out.

I go in after a little while. She's slumped over on the couch. Her eyes are closed. My parents are sitting there perched forward on their chairs like little birds. They look at me. We are all trying to act like this is normal.

"Augusta tells me she's reading *The Double Helix* for science class," my mother tells me.

What am I supposed to do now? Where's my Spock?

"Supper's ready," I tell them, and we all troop in.

But Augusta's got this down. "I can't eat. I told you, I'm sick."

So we all eat but Augusta.

She has her bare plate before her on the table.

"Not even some salad?" my mother asks her.

Augusta doesn't answer her. She glares at me. She sits facing me throughout the meal, glaring at me with her cold blue eyes. She's waiting. None of us can speak much during dinner. There is much fanfare with the sound of silverware on plates.

Then she says, "I have jazz band."

"I thought you were sick."

"I am, but I have to go or I'll get kicked out, he told me."

"We can take her," my father says. "We have to go right by there anyway."

She glares at me some more. "You," she says, meaning: *You take me,* meaning: *I have things to say to you in the car.* But I don't answer her. I look across her at my father.

"Fine," I say.

So they've had a glimpse. They get the picture. "How's she doing?" they ask me now by phone, and in my mind I see their worried faces.

"Not so good," I tell them, and then I try to think of something—something good I get to say. I tell them about work. I tell them about Jack playing on the baseball team. I tell them about my hike up Cadillac Mountain, but they're not fooled. I hear their heavy silence, and their pain.

I wasn't such a terrific kid myself. I know that now. But those were, as they say, different times—back when I was a teenager, back in the sixties. For one thing, the parents didn't know what was really going on. They didn't have a clue—because it was all so new—about drugs, about what we thought was a revolution. So they were spared some of what I am not, knowing exactly the danger, remembering the sensation, remembering the false, free feeling of immortality. I remember thinking it was fine to die, that dying was somehow another kind of wild adventure. Hallucinations!

Fantasy! Revenge! But not only that. It wasn't (I'm sure of this) as dangerous then as it is now. As dangerous to hitch-hike. As dangerous to go into strange houses. As dangerous to take drugs that people handed you in sunny meadows. Wasn't there—I can remember it—a camaraderie, a safe-ness, a closeness that's gone now? Or maybe it's just the way it seemed.

July 1969. I was seventeen. I remember hitchhiking to Ann Arbor with my friend Scott. We got picked up by a crowd in a big truck. We climbed up onto the big bed over the cab, stoned on acid, laughing as the road came hurtling toward us through the window. We were going to the blues festival. Same weekend as Woodstock.

Later, at a truck stop, I remember the big men turning around on their stools, staring. They couldn't tell us apart, the girls and the boys. We were a tribe. We were from an-other kingdom. All of us with our same long hair and our same bright, glittering, acid-bright eyes. We all looked the same to them. It was our camouflage. We were the outlaws.

And the feeling of the music later, lying on the grass, was tangible. You could lie back and get carried along by it, over the heaving crowd, out over the redwood snow fence. Out over the trees. I remember feeling invincible. Invincible, months later, driving over the Golden Gate Bridge in San Francisco in a big white car. The supports on either side left slanting shadows across the bridge in the clear morning light. I was going to Berkeley. I was going to Berkeley. I was gone.

That was a horrible time for my parents. I remember (be-cause she's often reminded me of it) my mother telling my sister in the backyard of our house in Washington, "I guess I just have to write her off. I guess I just have to give up on her."

But did she ever really say that? And did she ever really mean it? You don't get to give up on your kids. Forget tough love.

"What should I do?" I ask Bill, the vice principal and one of the few people I'll admit to.

"You might have to try tough love," he tells me. "Throw her out. Let her hit rock bottom."

But I can't do that. So I find myself playing by an odd set of made-up rules. It's like war. This is what my life has become. I am still pretending to myself that there are rules. And she is still pretending there are rules. And both of us know there are no rules left. In support of this pretense, and to stir up another fight, Augusta asks permission of me:

"I want to go over to Kyle's. We're going to watch a movie."

"It's a school night."

"I'll be home by ten."

"Nine."

"Fine. Nine."

She's home at ten thirty. I'm in bed. She rushes past my room so I can't see her face. Calls to me, supposedly with exhaustion, "Sorry I'm late. Kyle's car broke down. His mother had to drive us."

Nothing's true. But I'm exhausted. And so now what? What do I do now? Have a fight with her? Ground her? It's a joke. So I say, "Go to bed."

And so we have both behaved correctly, according to these weird rules.

According to the weird rules that I have devised respecting my children's privacy, I can search their rooms but I can't tell them what I find in their rooms. So when I find the grass and the pipe in her room, I don't tell Augusta. I'm even (I know this sounds insane) afraid to throw it out because then she'll know that I've betrayed her. What?

Meanwhile it escalates. In spite of all my precautions, all my careful attempts to hold some weird shaky line at some weird point: Okay, so she does go out on school nights, but has to be in by nine, well, Okay, ten if there's a car problem. Okay, she can't spend the night at boys' houses, but she can spend the night at girls' houses, but only if the parents are there and I speak to the parents. Okay, she can't smoke, but we both know she does smoke, but not in the house. Okay, we both know that she smokes in the house, but she does it with her door closed and her window open and I can't go in her room because the door is closed.

Okay, I don't yell, but she yells at me, but I don't back down nor do I yell because if I yell I'll go crazy and I'll never stop, but it's okay if she yells because she needs to.

And in spite of all of this the battle escalates. My forbearance makes her more furious. She screams at me. She screams at me from the doorway of my bedroom. She screams at me at the dinner table. At the breakfast table. She doesn't eat breakfast but she comes down to scream at me. She screams at me from her room, from outside the door of the bathroom, in the car, in the yard, in the living room. She screams at me when I am at my desk.

I am afraid of her. I don't even know anymore if I love her. There used to be those little windows, those little windows through which I saw my girl. But now I can't see anyone but this angry mean person. She hates me and I don't even know what I think about her. I'm supposed to keep her safe. I'm supposed to get her through school. I'm supposed to be her mother. I'm supposed to love her.

"But she's so mean," I say out loud to myself when I finally get out of the house and go walking. It's a pale spring evening. The roads of our town are full of women walking. They walk in pairs. They walk with their husbands. They walk with their dogs. I think I am the only woman who is walking alone, head down, talking to herself, saying softly to myself, "She's so mean."

Something must be done. I can't imagine it. I am scuttling from one day to the next day. I am waiting it out. It's a siege. Gone are all the vestiges. Gone my plans. The map's caught by the wind and flutters off over the battlements. The army's dead, the wounded lying all around me. Flags once flown brightly are tattered at their stands. I have forgotten my own name. Yet somehow, in all of this, I am getting up every morning at four forty-four. I am getting up, I am pulling on my slippers. I go down to my desk. I make the lunches. I make the coffee. I drink the coffee at my desk. I pull on my clothes and my sneakers and go for my walk early in the morning before all the other women are walking, before the long day. I go to work. I take the calls from the school. I go home. At night I go back out and search for her sometimes or sometimes I just wait up. I wait for her to leave when she is home. I wait for her to come home when she is out. I am her prisoner.

"I feel like a prisoner!" she yells at me. "I need to be free!" she screams at me.

"You never let me do anything!" she roars at me. She does anything she wants. But what she hates is that she knows she isn't supposed to.

It's such a quaint balance. It's fragile as a rickety old toy.

Looking back, of course, everything looks different. Looking back you see whatever finally came was always coming. It was always there.

6

I'm saying this all wrong. I want to get it right, be organized about it. Tell it straight. But the memories are so uneven and so jangled that I can't. I remember only little pieces of it and I remember some of the sensation. But it's like labor. Like labor with my daughter. Oy. She was terrible to give birth to—it should have been a warning. Three weeks late. In upside down. One false trip to the hospital and then another, longer stay. It took her twenty-six hours to make her appearance, after hours of waiting and writhing, after the water broke, the Pitocin was administered, the scraping unwilling lunge of her to come outside. My husband saying breathe breathe breathe at me. The nurses making their comfortable nurse jokes. The doctor telling me I'm getting some results. My own fury, pain, impatience with the whole medieval procedure. GIVE ME DRUGS I roared at them until finally, hours in, days in, they finally did.

So she was born. A beautiful, finally, a lovely girl. Immediately beautiful. Not like her brother with his skinny legs and patchy hair and uncertain little quizzical pirate's face looking out, but round-faced, blue-eyed, beige-haired, perfect perfect child. Healthy immediately and very strong and staring up at me, at first all slimy and later staring up out of her folded blanket exquisite, beautiful, my daughter.

And later, as they tell you, it was true, I didn't remember how much it had hurt. I remembered that it hurt. I remembered yelling with the pain. But I didn't remember the pain itself. And so, though I remember the disorientation, the exhaustion, the thickness of my pain as she deteriorated, as our house became a battleground, filled up with blood, I don't remember exactly, remember clearly, cleverly, remember the pain itself. How sad I was, how desperate, how lost.

And she was so sad too.

Later, when I try to tell her why we did what we did, I say, Augusta, look at me. I didn't send you there as a punishment. I sent you there because I couldn't help you. I couldn't save you. I was afraid you wouldn't survive. But it wasn't the drugs, it wasn't the stealing, the running out at night, the lying, any of that. It was your enormous unhappiness. It was that in the midst of those terrible fights, those awful, crazy, yelling furies of yours, you would start to cry, you would say—when I told you to do better at school, when I told you to try to get through jazz band, when I told you to look for a summer job—what you said was, "You don't understand. I'm no good. I'm no good. I'm no good."

And then I knew, when I saw you crying like that, when I saw you crying and yelling and so furious with rage and sorrow, I knew that I deserved all of your anger and your fury and your hatred because surely this was all my fault.

But I also knew that you had to be away from me. That was what I said out loud to myself on my walks that sad and furious winter, that straggly spring. That's what I said to those few friends I could still stand to see. That's what I said to my therapist. She has to get away from me. Because you had taken all of the darkness inside of yourself and smeared it on me. And I had become the reason for everything. I was your icon of wrongness. I was the one you could blame.

Summertime. Augusta was just two. I put her in her sunny room to nap after the long walk downtown. The long play-time in the morning at the playground.

"Take a little nap," I told her, putting her into her crib, and left the room.

When I came in a couple of hours later the room stank with shit. My daughter was curled up against her stuffed animals. Her dark shit was everywhere. Smeared on the crib, smeared on her hands and belly, smeared on the wall she could reach from between the bars of her crib. Her sheets. Her animals. All smeared with shit.

This happened again and again, for a year or so. And I reacted typically, badly, erratically, with everything from disgust to anger to controlled, quiet remonstrance. Which one worked? It finally ended.

But I remember clearly that stinking visit to the hot summer bedroom. The smell of shit. Her little face looking up at me from her filth.

There's one memory from the craziness that's like a little pool in a tangled woods. The last good time: my father's eightieth birthday. We are having a party. It's May. My sister and her family have come up from Washington. She's married to a doctor. They live in a house a lot like the house that we grew up in. Though she is older, her children are younger. Two little boys. And they are beautiful, wearing shorts, and they have chubby legs. They adore my older, monosyllabic children. Can't wait to see them! my sister tells me by e-mail. Can't wait!

"So we have to spend the whole weekend with them?" Augusta has already asked me.

"No," I've promised her, "but you do have to go to the party."

It's going to be in the daytime: Sunday. "Daisy's going to pick me up afterwards."

"Okay."

I am expecting another Christmas, another Easter. But the children actually seem glad to be going. Augusta and I are in and out of each other's rooms in the morning, admiring and criticizing each other's clothing.

"What do you think?" I stand back with a different shoe on each foot. "What do you think of these?"

"I think the brown ones," she tells me from the bed. "Definitely."

"What about the necklace?" I ask her.

"Don't even consider it," she tells me, in a quote that delights me. "It's Sunday, Mom! Get with it! That's a Thursday thing."

She looks so beautiful in her long velvet skirt and Indian print shirt. Her hair has gotten long and is already streaked with gold the way it gets in summer. Her eyes are so blue.

Jack's tall and uncomfortable with his huge pants and his

size-fifteen shoes. They look so wonderful I want to take their picture. But I don't push it.

While I'm brushing my teeth, they turn the music up loud in Augusta's room and dance together in the hallway.

Jack barely moves. He's ultracool. Six foot two and with his cap pulled down. Augusta, who abruptly stopped growing at five three, is dancing all around him like a little animal. Prancing five moves to his one. They love each other. We're a family.

I let her drive. She's got her permit now. She cranks the radio and I sit in the back and don't object.

My mother's gone all out. The table is set with party hats and noisemakers and favors and bright candy in ruffled baskets. The sun shines in.

We go out in the driveway, all of us, to take our family picture. My sister has an automatic camera but it doesn't work right and keeps taking snapshots of her behind as she runs back to get into the picture. Her youngest son gets mad and starts yelling. My brother-in-law tries to quiet him down. We're making snide remarks out of the corners of our mouths and all of us are laughing when the picture finally snaps.

Later, after dinner, Augusta lets one of the boys sit in her lap. She reads a story to the two of them, sitting on the couch with them. She's been good all day.

"She seems pretty good," my sister tells me in the kitchen.

I roll my eyes, but I believe it, too.

Daisy comes by for her at three o'clock. "Okay," I tell her. "You can go. Just make sure you tell your grandfather happy birthday."

She comes back into the room and surprises us and thrills us all by kissing him on the cheek.

"Thank you," she tells my mother.

She hugs the little boys.

We can see her from the window as she gets into the red convertible Daisy drives. Some relic from the seventies with the white top down.

The two pretty girls sail off, waving like girls in a movie long ago.

"They are so young," my mother says. "They have such a good time."

Then, without warning, she's missing for two days. This is a first. She calls once, muffled, but won't tell me where she is. "I need some time away," she says. "You always have to know everything."

She hasn't been to school.

"Will you excuse her?" Bill asks me. "If you don't she's going to be suspended."

I say okay.

"At least we know she's all right," my ex says on the phone.

"How do we know that?"

"She called you, didn't she?"

I call her friends.

I haven't slept.

I call her friends from work. I drive around. She could be anywhere. She could have gone to Boston. Who's she with?

"I really don't know. Honestly," Daisy tells me.

I believe her.

"We went to a party, that night? But then I left and she didn't want to come. She said she could get a ride home later. But I don't know now. It's been two days."

"You'll let me know if you hear anything from her?" I ask.

"Just tell her to come home, tell her she's not in trouble. Tell her to just come home."

I don't know if she's in trouble or she's not in trouble. I don't know where she is.

One night I'm crying, sitting up in bed. Jack stands in the doorway, useless and long limbed. He doesn't want to come into my room. I can see why. It's full of too much emotion.

"Think about something good," he tells me kindly, awkwardly, at last. "Think about chocolate chip cookie dough. That's what I do."

"Chocolate chip cookie dough?" I give him a creepy smile to show that I'm all right.

"How's Augusta?" my mother asks me, by telephone. "She looked so pretty the other day at Daddy's party. Wasn't that a nice party?"

"It was a beautiful party." That's all I say.

Augusta turns up the next night.

"I was worried about you," I tell her.

"I was fine," she says. "I'm hungry. Got anything to eat?"

And she ravages the rest of the chicken from the other night and grabs a bunch of cookies and eats them quickly one right after another at the kitchen table with a glass of juice.

"Can't you wait for supper?" I ask her. "Let's have dinner together."

"I'll still be hungry," she tells me. But of course she isn't.

She is in her room with the music up loud when Jack and I eat later.

They are in his room until late talking. When I knock on the door they tell me go away.

❦

"We need to talk," I tell my daughter. I almost say *young lady* like a mother in a television show.

It's a few days later. She's been going to school. She says she's been doing her work.

"Okay," she tells me. "But does it have to be long?"

"No. It doesn't have to be long," I tell her. "But we have to talk."

So we go into my room and we both sit on my bed.

"This is too crazy, the way we are going on right now."

"What's wrong?" she asks me, like there's nothing.

"You need to go to school every day. You need to do your work. You need to be home on time. You need to not take drugs or smoke and you need to tell me where you are."

She rolls her eyes. She's waiting this one out.

"I can't do that." She shakes her head. "You want me to be honest with you, so I'm telling you that. I'm almost sixteen. I need to have freedom. I do go to school, but I have to see my friends. I can't always tell you where I'm going to be, 'cause I don't know. You should understand. You were like me."

"I wasn't quite like you," I tell her.

This is how it starts out but this isn't the way it ends up. Her voice goes up and up until it's too high, too loud, and I can't talk. I'm stuck back, stuck into the bed, pinned there.

She wants to be free. She wants to be on her own. Someday she's just going to run away and then I won't have any idea where she is. Someday she's just going to take off. If she had her license, she'd be gone now. Her friends are coming over in a little while, can she go now?

"I'm staying at Jude's," she tells me. "Rain and I."

Jude is twenty-four and goes to the College of the Atlantic, which makes her seem to Augusta somehow more daring and more intelligent than other women.

I find Jude in the video store where she works part-time.

"I wanted to meet you," I tell her. "I'm Augusta's mother."

"Oh yeah right."

She's small and dark and intense looking, the kind of girl I knew when I was twenty-four.

"She's really cool, Augusta. She's a cool girl."

What does that mean? Attractive? Smart?

"She's only fifteen," I tell Jude now. "You have to remember that. She's just a kid."

"Oh I know, but she knows a lot. She's very deep."

"Yeah, she's deep, and she's smart, but she's young. Sometimes you can get confused by her and taken in and think she's older than she is. She thinks she's older. But when she stays with you, you need to keep an eye on her."

"Oh I do. We don't do much. I mean, I'm not exactly wild. We watch movies. We hang out. I do my art and she and Rain like to fool around in the studio. I think they can relate to me. They can't relate to school. They're too cool for it. They relate to me because I hated school too. I dropped out."

"And you're in college now?"

"Yeah. It was the best thing I ever did. Dropping out."

I'm up against it. My own past and my fearful mother-hood.

I've given up on cool. I'm not cool. Not in the old way. But I know that school's dumb. I hated school. I remember sitting in the classroom thinking dumb dumb dumb. Dumb classes about dumb things taught by dumb people. And I am dumb with disappointment. Dumb with dread.

"So she'll be spending the night at your house tonight?"

"Yep."

"Remember, she's fifteen. She has to be in by midnight if she goes out, and you have to know where she's going."

"Sure. I will. I'll look after her."

She doesn't seem like a bad girl, I tell myself. I tell myself she has a job. She's going to college. She's kind.

And anyway, what am I supposed to do? Isn't this better than nothing?

7

I TAKE A WALK UP Schoolhouse Ledge. It's a quiet evening. It will be light for hours. In another month or so I won't be able to come up here. The summer people will be here and it will be off-limits. I walk purposefully up the road with the wet spring woods on either side. The moss seems greener now, the houses fresher. The trunks of the trees are bright black and everything looks new.

At the top I do my prayer from the big rock: stand up on it and hold my arms out, looking out over the hillsides of the mountains. The water of the Sound. The sky. The last late sun. I go up the stone porch of the big house and look in the windows the way I like to look in the windows there. I imagine walking through those rooms. I imagine that I could go into those rooms and become another person. My life transformed. But of course it's not so.

Evening. It's finally dark. I go to bed. There are no phone calls. There are no messages. I go to sleep.

In the morning I'm up early.

I expect a phone call from my daughter, needing a ride home from Jude's. I spend some time at my desk. It's Sunday morning. It's the day I plan my whole week out. Make a list of things I want to accomplish. So many things to do! I feel purposeful and proud. The day is cloudy but it didn't rain last night and this morning there are watery streaks of blue sky with the clouds. I think it might clear off enough to climb a mountain. Sunday. May. It's Mother's Day. They might make me a card—last year they did—or even supper.

A truck pulls up to the house. I can't see the driver's face with the reflection. It's a truck I don't know. Blue. New. High up off the ground.

My daughter hops out of the passenger side, runs up the driveway. The truck moves off. I can't see who it is.

She comes in the door. She has bare feet. She's dirty. She looks as if she's run through the woods all night. She's got her old pants on and her old sweater. Her hair's all tangled. She looks weird, tired. Creaky almost, pale.

"I wanted to come home for Mother's Day," she says.

"Are you okay? Who gave you a ride home?"

"That was Dusty. He came by Jude's for me. To bring me home."

"Where were you?"

"I told you. Jude's. I've got to have a shower."

She brushes by me and goes up the stairs.

I stand around waiting. I was just about to go out when she came in.

Nine thirty. It's early for her to come home.

She takes an endless shower.

I hear her tramp across the hall into her room.

"I'm going to sleep now," she yells down to me. "I need to sleep."

"I might go out," I tell her.

"Okay," she calls down, faintly, from her room.

When I go up, look in on her, she's lying on her bed. She's reading one of the books she likes to read now—some paperback she liked when she was twelve. She who was always the amazing reader, far ahead of her years with books, is back to *Baby-Sitters Club.* and R. L. Stine. Back to the easy, matching series books she always used to scorn. She reads them over and over in the same way she eats, furiously, hungrily, hungry for oblivion—like me.

"Are you okay?" I ask her, standing in the doorway of her room.

"I'm fine," she answers me. "I told you, I'm just tired. I'll probably hang out here, take a nap," she says.

"I'm going to go climb a mountain. Want to come?"

She looks at me. "You kidding?"

I go up Day Mountain fast, furiously. Up the spring mountain. Climbing wet rocks past black trunks and bright sky overhead and up, moving fast, liking the turbulence of the climb, liking the hardness of it: the true, new ache in winterlogged limbs. The good strength. While I'm hiking I let my thoughts go. It's like listening to music. At first I'm aware of the orchestra itself. Of the different players, of the audience around me, of my clothes. But then I go past all of that, go up with the music, up with the mountain, up out of my own self and my own regrets, up into the sky. Bits of thoughts like old rags fling about me. I could, if I wanted to, reach out and snag a piece of paper with a word on it. A word like "memory" or a word like "dusty" or a name.

That's when I discover my thoughts; when I stop thinking. And it's on the mountain that I recognize my odd unease. The way she looked. The dirty feet. The eyes, the tiredness remind me of another time, another tired girl, another morning.

June 1969. I've been kicked out of school for smoking pot. Kicked out in March. Finished my senior year at home with a tutor. Got into college—well, Antioch, what do you expect?—and got prepared to go. But despite my mother's pleas, despite my letter, the headmistress of my very narrow all-girls prep school said I couldn't graduate with my class.

I'd sort of always dreaded graduation, just as my mother had longed for it. It was a very old-fashioned school and they had a graduation ritual that was right up my mother's alley, and sort of up mine, in spite of what I had lately become—a dirty girl in jeans with ragged hair. A girl in poncho and cowboy boots. A girl with cigarettes who said *fuck* every other word (but not around grown-ups, not on the bus). A girl who snuck out of her house at night and might be seen hitchhiking around Washington, D.C., at 2 A.M. (what was I thinking?). But there was still that other side of me. The princess side. The fairy-tale dilemma. The candy-box bedroom.

All the fifty girls of the class would be dressed in white dresses. We would be paraded down a pathway to a sylvan glade. The Amphitheater, as it was called, nestled in the Virginia woods that surrounded the hockey-fielded, horse-paddocked, old ivy-and-brick, curving-asphalt bower of our school. It was, incidentally, in this very glade one early spring afternoon that Veronica Hardsdale and I had smoked the marijuana that had gotten us kicked out of Madeira in the first place.

Anyway. My mother had been hoping that since I had managed in the privacy of my boudoir to finish all my work for school with better than passing grades, I would be allowed to don the white dress, carry the red roses, and parade with the other misshapen girls of my class down the wide green swath cut carefully for this one day a year, emerge virginal, but with the passionate red roses, out of the springtime woods and stand, shorn head bowed, with the others during the interminable speech by some successful tycoon father of a student dragged for the occasion into the murky Virginia June woods humid with hormones and heat while the Victrola played and we were all sent out from this, our pristine past, into the harsher, grim reality of life. But they wouldn't let me.

The hardened old polo-coated battle-ax who was headmistress of the school refused to let me, in spite of my letter grudgingly written at my mother's sad behest. In spite of my mother's tearful meeting with her in her brown plaid office.

("Haven't you punished her enough? Won't you let her walk with the other girls? Won't you let her carry those red roses?")

My mother was not one to give up easily and so she, like a sad dog with a bone in its mouth, worried and worried at the bone of my graduation. But to no avail.

On the morning of what would have been my graduation, my sister and I persuaded our mother to go out of town with us. My father was away, as I recall, and it was just us three. My sister home, successfully, from Smith, and on her way for a continental tour and for what was to turn out to be a year in Paris. I'd finished my work and it was a hot—a boiling sunny hot—clear day in June. And I remembered thinking gladly, fiercely glad, how uncomfortable all those girls were going to be in their itchy white dresses standing in the woods with all the chiggers and mosquitoes and the like, clutching their spiny, limply hanging bundles of old roses anyway. But still.

So the three of us went off in our yellow Volkswagen with the top down and, I remember, drove around the country-side of Pennsylvania—Amish country—stopping for lunch with lemonade at a little inn, browsing in antique stores, eating ice cream. I fell asleep in the backseat on the way home and got a terrible sunburn. But it was somehow grand. We got along that day. That day, I think, was the day I remembered how to love my mother.

That night I went out with my friends. There was a party. It was one of those strange and confusing nights with lots of acid. I wound up later at home, my sister sleeping, innocently sleeping, in her bed. My mother in her bed sleeping, sleeping. And I, sitting up in my room, stoned on acid, distracted by the twirling blue snowflakes on the blue-and-white patterned wallpaper of my girlhood bedroom. Flouncy flouncy curtains billowing, but in this vision, LSD-enhanced, not just billowing but bulbously and somehow hideously swollen bunching out at me their gossamer bellies which I'd been told once were made of spun glass and which I always thought might cut me if they brushed by chance—those billowing dangerous bellies—against my face.

So there I was trapped on a summer evening in my room. The twirling wallpaper, the billowing bellies. The snores of my sister and my mother vibrating the walls of the house where I had always always lived.

I did what I inevitably did. What my own daughter would do, years later. I snuck out.

I had a system in those days. I'd crafted it carefully, and I was rather pleased with my handiwork. The careful plan of my escape.

First, listen.

Crouching on my bed. Listen, listen.

Nothing?

Okay. Out of the bed, normally, making normal sounds. Normal enough but not too noisy, not to wake them, but normal so if they are awake (if they, too, are lying in their twirling beds alert and sleepless as my mother always might be) and if they hear me it's not odd.

I was already dressed, but for my shoes (for who, even I, even raggedy haired as I was, a total rebel, could possibly put her big shod feet into her own, her clean white sheets?).

So, shoes in hand, I went to the door of my room. Hyperalert and listening for sounds. Open the door (again normally—not loudly! normally) and then to the bathroom, where I made appropriate gestures simulating a period of urination, no clothes time because supposedly I was in nightclothes, then flush the toilet, run the water, listen, back out into the hall and toward my room—but wait! Here's the crafty part! Not *into* my room—just *toward* my room—and then I shut the bedroom door, but from the *outside*. Then down the hall and down the stairs. I knew where the stairs creaked. I knew which ones. I knew to walk on the outside of the treads. Careful careful careful. Always listening. Always alert.

If only I had used that cleverness that bravery that daring for something useful. All my life. How much I could have made of it! Oh well.

But then, seventeen, stoned, at the bottom of the stairs. Unlock the door. The chain first. Don't let it drop down, fall against the door. The navel of the doorknob next, the turning of the knob. All done in utter silence. Then open the door. Only a little, because at about sixty-five degrees it starts to screek. Slip out. Close the door. Don't get cocky now. Close the door silently and pull it shut. Stand a moment, listening, listening, and then—now don't get cocky!—down the stairs. One stair, the other, one more, two. The sidewalk and you feel that jumping leap, that lively, light-stepped fantasy—the night!

The big full trees above! The streetlight and the carless silent nighttime center of the nighttime street.

Oh then we had adventures! Then we wailed! We went to late-night parties on the other side of town. We drove around, drove far into the country in a "borrowed" car. We sat in smoky houses full of strangers listening to music, acting old so nobody would ask us who we were.

But that night, the night after the day that should have been my graduation, that night I went only around the corner, only down the block, to Brendan's house to spend the night with him.

His parents were away and we were lovers. And though we'd "done it" several times we hadn't ever really slept together. So this was another magic stoned adventure. I wasn't sure I liked what we were doing. His pale white body and his milky skin. I wasn't sure I liked him, even. But it didn't matter. It was really *bad*.

We slept in his mother's bed. The idea was that we would have sex, only doze, and then I'd sneak away and go back home in a couple of hours.

That was the idea.

But of course, once the LSD wore off, we were exhausted. And what with sex and all, we fell asleep.

I woke up. It was already getting light.

I jumped out of bed.

"I have to go," I told him.

"Wha?" he remarked.

He looked terrible in the gray light. Like a baby with his slitty eyes and acne and his frowsy hair. And his mother's room was nothing like my mother's room. I felt grouchy and disoriented and dirty. I left the house.

The street didn't feel so secret in the light. I felt scared, but not scared in the glittery way of the night before. My fear this time was like a cold gray stone.

The house looked different as I came upon it in the morning light. It rose up from its front porch like my mother's face.

The door was locked. I stole around the back. Crouching by the back porch, I peered in. I could see my mother walking in the kitchen. Wearing her mommy bathrobe. Fixing coffee. She had the newspaper. She headed up the stairs.

I ran back to Brendan's house.

"I need some clothes!"

I woke him up.

"My mother's awake. I need some clothes."

"What clothes?"

"This is what I wore last night. I can't go back in these."

He was still half awake. He looked stupid.

I started looking in, of all places, his mother's closet.

"What the fuck are you doing?" he asked me like a fussy principal.

"Looking for clothes," I told him, turning around, helpless, frightened, at the closet. "I told you. I have to have on different clothes."

"Well, you can't go in my mother's closet! Get the fuck out of there."

Oh I hated him.

"Fine. What am I supposed to do?"

"I don't know."

He fell back on the bed and pulled a grayish pillow over his face. He was a fine one.

I stood there staring at him. We were more like siblings than lovers.

Finally he put off the pillow, sat up. "All right. I'll find you something. But not in my mother's closet, for fuck's sake. I think there's something upstairs, some pants my sister borrowed from Rosie."

"They'll be too small."

"She's pretty fat," he said.

I got the pants on. I borrowed a shirt from him.

I went back through the now wide awake Sunday-morning streets.

Miraculously the door wasn't locked. It had just been stuck.

I went in boldly with my new clothes, boldly went upstairs.

"Hi Mom," I said from the hallway to where she lay in bed with her glasses on, coffee on the bedside table, reading the Sunday paper.

She looked at me but I couldn't see her eyes. The light reflected off her glasses and I couldn't see her expression. She just lay there and suddenly I felt sorry for her. Sorry for being such a terrible daughter. Sorry for getting kicked out of school. Sorry for the roses and the lies.

"I went for a walk," I told her, giving her the story I'd concocted on my way home from Brendan's, second trip.

"Oh?" she said lifelessly.

"Leo came by this morning and asked me if I wanted to go for an early walk."

She didn't believe me. She didn't say anything.

"So we went on a walk. I'm tired. I'm going back to sleep."

"Okay," she told me. But she didn't believe me. And it

scared me, not because she didn't believe me. It scared me because she didn't seem to care.

I think about this now, climbing Day Mountain on Mother's Day morning almost thirty years later.

This morning with my daughter was eerily like that morning long ago. Only now I'm my mother and I still do care and I see that my mother cared back then, still cared. But I feel as futile as she must have felt. As hopeless and as helpless and as lost, with all her faults and mistakes parading before her as she tried to figure out what she'd done wrong.

You want to push away your daughter when it gets like that. Because there's too much self-reproach in seeing her stoned, lying, dirty, lost. The kind of girl you never meant to have. And it seems as if she is the daughter that you most deserve. So you want to push her away. Get her out of your life. So you don't have to see what you've done wrong.

8

WHO AM I KIDDING? There is something wrong. She was stoned on acid. I know that look. That's what I recognized. I know that look. I used to have it too.

I get back to the trail down and I practically run down the mountain over the rocks and ridges. Get into my car, drive over to Bar Harbor, walk right into the video store where Jude works. She's behind the counter.

"Where was Augusta last night?"

"She stayed at my house."

She looks at me with that same baleful look my daughter gives me. That same hooded look, that same distrust. She's on the other side of the divide still. She hasn't yet had children.

"Please tell me what really happened."

I look at her. Inside her face there's a good girl. I can tell it. She might even be Catholic. I win because I'm not screaming at her. I win with power.

"She didn't stay at my house," she tells me finally, heavily.

"She started out there. Then she and Rain went to a party. I don't know where. Somewhere on the Backside of the Island. I guess there were a lot of people there. And there was some stuff going on. So Rain didn't like it. She wanted to leave, but Augusta wouldn't leave, and Rain didn't want to leave her there, so she kept trying to get Augusta to leave. This is just what I heard."

She pauses.

"I guess the cops came. And some of the kids went into the woods. I don't think it was all kids. I think there were some older people there. Anyway, some of them went into the woods, and then there was some fighting. And a few people got hurt. I don't really know what happened. Rain left. She got a ride or something. She came back to my place. It was really late. I don't know where Augusta went. Did she get home?"

"She's home now. She came in this morning," I tell Jude.

"Well, don't blame her too much. I mean, they need to go through this stuff. They need to find their way. Augusta's got a good head on her shoulders. She's careful who she goes with. What she takes. I mean, she does take stuff, you know that."

"What do you mean, stuff?"

A person comes into the store. Starts browsing in the movies. Funny. Action. Horror. Love.

I lower my voice, stare right into Jude's little face.

"What kind of stuff?"

"Well you know. She's done some 'shrooms. You know that, don't you?"

"I guessed." I feel sick. It's here now. It's before me.

"They all do. I've done them. It's no big deal, if you're with good people. I always make sure they're safe if they're with me. And Augusta is really careful about who she guides

83

with. Rain is really serious about it. She won't let Augusta get hurt. But you know, they have their path."

"But what if they do get hurt?"

I stare at her. I forget about the other person in the store, looking at the boxes boxes boxes.

"I'm her mother. It's my job to keep her safe. It's my job to stop her when she's doing stuff that could hurt her. Don't you see? I love her. I want her to survive this time in her life. So what if she's careful? She doesn't even know—I bet she doesn't even know what she's taking!"

"But what are you going to do?" Jude asks me. Not in a cruel way. Just asks me.

"What are you going to do about it, really? It's her life. She's going to do certain things. And you can try to stop her. But it won't work. I mean, school's a joke, and she can see that. And she wants to explore certain things. She's going to do it. If you try to stop her, she'll leave."

"Did she say she would?"

"Believe me. *I* did. She will."

The person comes up to the counter. It's a woman. Probably about twenty-five. She's got a horror movie and I try to picture who would choose a movie with a baby on the cover with a knife dripping blood on a Sunday morning in May, Mother's Day in May when the first, new, watery blue sky of the spring is here. I look at her and she looks so regular. Brown hair, regular eyes, a jacket. She probably is regular. This is probably normal.

She pays for the movie and waits while Jude locates it on the shelves full of blue plastic cases.

"Here you go," says Jude, like a waitress with a plate of eggs and sausage.

"Thanks," the woman says. And she goes out.

"I better go," I tell Jude.

"Don't tell her I told you that," Jude tells me. "She thinks I'm her friend. She really trusts me."

I think of saying something—I almost do say something like: You *are* her friend. A true friend takes care of her friends, helps keep them safe—but it would sound too corny and I doubt she'd get it. So I just say thank you and assure her I won't tell and I go out.

Groceries. I can get a lot of groceries. She's probably hungry. Fresh fruit. Big salad stuff. Nice loaves of bread. She likes Double Stuf Oreos. I get those. She likes cranberry juice cocktail, so I get that, too. Lemon Popsicles, the expensive kind, six to a box that says "Limited Edition" in a very snappy black-and-yellow. She will love those. Maybe she'll stay home and eat them. I get frozen juice and frozen pizza and mangoes even though they're not on sale. Dried apricots. Sugary cereal in the shape of tiny French toasts. Hot salsa. Blue-corn chips. Whatever I can woo her with, whatever I can please her with. So that when I come into the kitchen with the heavy bags she will reach inside and pull things out and look so glad so happy so delighted and it will be I who have delighted her. I who have provided for her. I who bring home the Pop-Tarts and the juice!

She's still asleep when I get home.

I unpack the car and put the groceries away. Jack's been home and left again on a long bike ride through the woods with Josh. He's left a note for me: *Be home for supper.*

Late in the afternoon I hear her padding around upstairs. Into the bathroom, pad pad pad. The toilet flushing. Back to her room. From her doorway a little call to me: "Ma?"

"Hi honey," I call up to her.

"Oh." That's it. She goes into her room.

I wait a little, weighing the way to best approach her. I
don't want to fight with her. I want to go beyond this. I know
now that I only want to keep her. Do what it takes. Jude's
right in a sad way. She is going to do what she will do. She
could leave. I need to make her remember that she loves me.
I need to make her want to stay here. At least we can have
some semblance of safety. At least some of the time she can
be safe. But it has to start with her telling me some truths.

I go upstairs.

I go into her room. I'm not allowed there.

"Hi, honey."

She's lying on her bed. "What time is it?"

"It's almost four o'clock."

We look at each other. She's considering how much I
might have figured out, how much I know.

"Augusta. I want you to tell me where you were last night.
I know you weren't at Jude's."

I say this quickly so she won't start out by lying right away.

At last she talks to me: "I did go to Jude's. Rain and I
went. But there was this party. I told Jude where we were going. At the quarry. Dusty gave us a ride over. Dusty and
Kyle. They're good drivers.

"It was fun. There were lots of people there, but Rain
didn't like it. She kept wanting to go, but I didn't want to go.
All of my friends were there. Plus some people I didn't
know. Scary people. But I stayed with my friends."

"Was there drinking?"

"Some people were drinking. I don't drink. I told you. It's
disgusting. I don't drink. So anyway, somebody started making too much noise or something, I don't know, we were way
on the other side. But then somebody said everybody had to
leave. The cops were coming or something, so people started

getting into trucks and cars and trying to go out but the road was blocked you know with cops so we had to go back in. I wasn't there. I was on the other side the whole time, but I heard them yelling. So then I ran with a bunch of other people—Dusty, Kyle, somebody else, Annie—and we ran into the woods. That's when I lost my shoes. And we hid in the woods way in and it was wet and really dark but it was kind of fun. You know? It's fun when you do things like that, you know—hiding in the woods. But it was scary too and we had to be really quiet and there were people yelling for us but we couldn't really hear them. Then, after a long time, when it calmed down, we came out. And Rain was gone and Annie had gotten hit in the head with a beer can and had an asthma attack and somebody had to take her to the hospital so everybody was all upset. It was really late by then. I don't know what time. Really late. So it was too late for Daisy and me to go home so she and I went to Dusty's and we slept there."

She stops.

"His mother was there and his little sister and Daisy and I slept together on a mattress on the floor. So it was fine.

"And then this morning I made him take me right home. You promised me I wouldn't be in trouble if I told you."

"I know I did. You're not in trouble."

I'm trying to make sense of all of this. I'm trying to put my mind around all the parts that bother me. The older people—losers in their twenties, guys from Bangor driving down to the Island to party. The beer. Somebody hit in the head with a beer can. The asthma attack. The spectacle of the quarry with the trucks turned to shine their headlights on the bobbing crowd. The shadows of the quarry and the deep ravine. The huddled groups, the younger kids, crouching together on the far side of the quarry smoking joints. The cops.

Kids running around in the darkness. Augusta running into the woods barefoot, stoned, over the rocks and roots. Off trail. Cutting her feet on things, bashing past wet branches.

"You're not in trouble," I tell her now, in her bedroom. "But this isn't what I want you to do."

"I knew it!" she tells me. "I knew you'd say that, or something like that. You don't let me have a life. These are my friends. They didn't do anything wrong. I didn't do anything wrong. I was just having fun."

I put my hands up.

"We need to talk about something," I tell her.

"What?"

"You need a job for this summer. I want you to make a list of things you might do and start looking this week. I'll help you. But I don't want you to just hang around all summer."

"I don't know what to do. I wanted to work at the ticket booth, but they won't hire me."

"Well, then you have to find something else."

"I don't know what."

"I know a couple of things. Let's make a list."

"All right. You go downstairs. I'll come down in a minute. And we'll talk about it."

"Okay," I say.

She looks sulky to me but not explosive. I judge her moods in various tones and levels of danger. But right now I feel I have the upper hand. She's subdued, tired from her big night, and a little ashamed because she hasn't really told me the whole truth. She has told me the truth the way she is good at telling it—telling enough of it that it seems plausible. Enough truth to get my attention and my grudging trust. I go downstairs.

In a little while she comes down. I'm in the kitchen. I am making soup. She sits down at the table. In the five minutes since I talked with her in her room there's been a change. She's furious and sullen, silent now.

"Fine," she tells me. "What do I have to do?"

I hand her a paper and a pen. "Write down things you might be able to do."

"I don't want to do anything."

"I'll write it down."

I sit down with her at the kitchen table. I write at the top of the page, *Augusta: Summer Jobs.* She glares at me.

"Okay. You can waitress at the Docksider."

"I don't want to."

"But you can. You have to have a job." I look at her with blank eyes. I hate myself this way. I write it down. "You can work at the studio."

"I don't think she'll hire me."

"But you can ask her." I write that down, too.

I'm just heading for another dead-end deal when she starts to cry.

"I can't do any of these things. You don't understand. I can't. I can't waitress. I get too confused. I can't work at the studio. She'll make me stretch canvases. I don't know how."

I put the pen down. I don't know what to do with her sorrow. It's in the way.

"You can, Augusta," I tell her. "You can learn. Look, I'll help you."

"No!" She's crying harder now. "You don't understand! I'm not like you! I'm not perfect! I can't do it! I can't just do a job like you can. You don't understand because you can always do everything! I can't. I'm no good! I'm no good!"

"You're great!" I tell her. "You're really smart. And you're so pretty and everybody always loves you. You can do anything."

"No I can't! No!"

She's crying harder now. She's yelling at me.

"I don't want a job like you! I don't want to work in an office. I don't want to belong to Rotary!"

"You think I do? You think I started out like this? You have to work! You have to work. Everybody has to. It's just how it is."

"I don't care! I'm only fifteen! I don't care!"

She gets up, yelling at me. I try to keep her with me at the table but she's screaming at me now, out of control entirely, red faced and streaming eyes. I stand up too and put my hands on her shoulders.

"You don't just get to go to parties and get stoned and hang out!" I tell her. I'm yelling too, now. "You have to *do* something."

"I can't!" she shouts, and writhes away from me. And runs upstairs and slams the door. Again.

She hates me. I sit down. I'm trembling. I sit at the kitchen table and I can hear her crying and yelling loudly in her room.

Later, in a phone call to one of her friends, this will turn into something else. I will have dug my fingernails into her shoulders. I will have clawed at her. I will have screamed in her face. And I will overhear a piece of it and I will wonder: Did I do that? And it will always be like this, terrible like this, and she will always hate me and I will always do the wrong thing, the wrong thing, the wrong thing.

9

JACK COMES HOME at suppertime. "Where's Augusta?"
"She's in her room."

He doesn't say anything else. He's got the story. He tells me he's going to supper down at Sean's. I don't blame him. So what if it's Mother's Day? All the more reason to stay away from this boiling house.

I move through the rooms with their late light. It's quiet now upstairs. She's been in my room, talking on the phone. There has been music on, too loud, and then no music.

I have eaten something, I guess. I guess I finished making the soup.

I have called Marie, who lives far away now, and told her about Augusta. "Just hang in there," she tells me. She has no children of her own. And if she did, they wouldn't be like this.

About seven o'clock Augusta comes downstairs. She is carrying a brown suede bag that used to be mine. I carried it when I was fifteen. She is wearing the rings I used to wear. She looks tiny and determined and quite calm.

"I'm going to Rain's," she tells me.

"It's a school night," I say.

"I need to."

"No. You can't go out."

"I'm going. They're meeting me at the library. They're giving me a ride."

"Who?"

"Rain and Sylvan."

"No."

"I'm going, Mommy. I'll go to school. We're staying at her dad's."

"You can't go."

"I have to go," she tells me and goes out the door.

I run after her. I grab her in the driveway like a dream. I have my hands on her shoulders; I turn her facing me. "You can't go," I tell her. I feel full of energy and light. "No."

"Get your fucking hands off me," she says. "I'm going now. Get the fuck off me."

"No." I'm almost giggling. I won't let her go. Not this time. Not ever.

"It's not funny!" she screams at me. "I'm going! Fuck you!"

"No. You can't go."

She screams and swears at me. And I am dimly aware of the neighbors who might be listening, and the cars that might go by, and the house behind me, as we stand in the driveway grappling. I'm bigger than she is. I am stronger than she is. I am holding her by the wrists. She twists around and swears and spits at me. And I am trying to think of a plan. Thinking what? I'm going to stand here holding her by the wrists all night? Holding her, trying to keep her from leaving all night? And all the next night? And all the rest of our lives holding her by her wrists in the driveway?

"You're taking my things with you. You can't take my things. That's my ring. That's my bag."

Amazingly, she stops. Yanks off the ring and throws it on the ground. "Fine," she says. "Fuck you," she tells me, and she runs into the house. And runs upstairs.

I follow her in. I hear her upstairs rummaging around for another bag. I hurry to the phone and call the police. I get the number wrong. I have to dial again. Then finally they answer.

I say, "Send someone to my house. My daughter's leaving."

Just as I hang up she's down the stairs and headed for the door, with her Guatemalan bag instead.

"It's mine!" she tells me. "Any complaints?" she asks.

Again I almost start to giggle. I want her to giggle with me. Don't we both know this is silly? It's all so crazy, all so ridiculous. She's my Augusta! She's my girl!

But I can't touch her. I can't reach her. I can't find her behind her craziness and fury. She stamps out and I stamp out after her.

We walk together down the driveway arguing. This time I don't try to grab her. But I try to slow her down, arguing with her. Arguing life arguments. Arguing about school. Arguing about responsibility. Trying to engage her. Trying to get her to stop, to turn, to stare at me, insult me, argue with me, anything, delay her. The police are coming. The police are coming. Surely they will come and keep her home.

But we are halfway up the street when the police car finally glides toward us through the coming evening. It's not Officer Harper as I had hoped, but a young one, Roy, who is kind and young and ineffectual and scared.

"What's going on?" he asks us, getting out of the car. "What's all this about?" Trying to sound hearty.

"You called the cops?" She looks around at me. "I can't believe this. This is so pitiful."

"I didn't know what else to do," I say.

"Augusta wants to leave," I tell him. "She can't go. She needs to go home."

He's very young. He reminds me suddenly of Jack, but a goonier, goofier Jack.

"You need to go home with Mum," he tells my daughter.

"No I don't," she says. "I'm leaving. I don't believe this. This is so fucking pitiful."

"What's pitiful?" he asks her.

"This. You. I have no respect for you. I just want you to know. I'm not fucking going home. I told her I'd go to school tomorrow. I have a place to be. I can't believe I'm even talking to you."

"You need to go home, young lady. This is Mother's Day. Is this any way to treat your mother?"

He's getting it all wrong, God bless him. But I'm shaking too hard to talk. I don't know what I can say that's any better.

Just then Sylvan and Rain drive up in his old VW bug. Rain has wrapped a turban of some sort around her head. She's wearing, as I remember later, robes. Maybe she's in a costume, I think dully. She sweeps out of the car and I am impressed that she hasn't caught any of her fluttering fabric on the door. She rushes to us.

"What's going on?" she says with her concerned face.

"Who's this?" the cop says.

"Rain," I say.

"My friend," Augusta says.

"I don't think this concerns you," the cop says to Rain.

"What concerns Augusta concerns me," she proclaims with great dignity. She's in her peace march mode. The girls have been protesting this spring at Bath. Kneel. Silent vigil. They can't touch us. Chant.

"Look, Rain," I say to her, "Augusta needs to come home. She was out all last night. She's got school tomorrow."

"School!" Rain says it like she's saying "Shit!"

"Yes. Unlike you, Augusta is still in school. And she needs to be in her home tonight."

"No I don't, Mommy," says Augusta in her angry voice. "I'm leaving. Don't you get it? You can bring in your cops and your soldiers—anything—but I'm not staying home tonight."

She and the cop get into further argument/discussion, while Rain turns her turbaned head to me. "I know how you're feeling. It's really hard." Her voice is suave.

"You don't know how I'm feeling," I say roughly. "Don't tell me you know how I'm feeling."

She looks at me with calm patience. "I do know, Martha."

"No you don't. You try raising a child. Having a baby. Carrying her nine months. You try to do everything right. Work hard to give her things she wants. Try to be a good parent even when it's hard. And then have that child turn on you and scream in your face. You do that and then tell me that you understand what I'm going through. You don't know anything."

"Wow," says Rain. "This is really intense," she tells me.

I want to smack her.

Now she turns to Augusta and Sylvan, who probably feels as useless and ridiculous as the cop does. He's just a young guy with lip rings that look too heavy for his face. They pull down his lower lip a little, giving him an expression as if he were about to cry. Now the three friends go a little way off and sit on the grass together. They are communing.

It's going to be dark soon. The sky is getting darker. It will be harder in the dark. I have searched before in the dark to find my daughter.

95

I say to the policeman, "Call her father. Get her father down here."

"Okay," he says. "I'll call the dispatcher. I'll be honest with you. I don't know what I can do here, Martha. I'll call the dispatcher and have them contact Ben. And I'll find out what her rights are."

He gets into his cop car and talks awhile, heatedly, on his car radio. The three kids are still sitting cross-legged in the grass. They're talking earnestly to one another. They don't seem interested in what we're doing. Just then Jack comes down the road on his bicycle. He sees the cop car and me standing there, and Sylvan's car.

"What's going on?" he asks me.

"We're over here!" Augusta calls to him from the grass. "Mommy's trying to get me arrested."

He looks at me in disbelief and then goes over to join the other kids.

The young cop is still sitting halfway inside his cop car, listening on his cell phone.

I walk over to the opened door. I'm still shaking.

"Can't you do something?" I ask him.

"Ben's on his way," he tells me, like that's something.

He gets out of the car. It's like he has a death to explain to me and doesn't want to. He's too young for this. Two years ago he was probably fighting with *his* mother.

"Here's the thing. I don't know what—how much—I can do. Let me ask you this—do you think she's a danger to herself or to anyone—say, to you?"

"Not really."

"Was she talking about killing herself?"

"She has, but I don't think seriously."

"How about threats? Has she threatened you?"

"No."

"See, here's the thing, Martha, if she's a threat to anyone, even herself, we can hospitalize her."

"I don't want to hospitalize her!"

"Right. So the other thing is, we can hold her for six hours. At the police station."

"Okay."

"Yeah, but then we have to release her to the state."

"You mean you can't make her come home?"

"We could take her home, but she'll just run. Tonight. Tomorrow. Sometime."

"So what can I do?"

"Well, we can put her in the hospital if you think she's endangering herself, we can take her to the station, but then she goes into state custody, or you can let her go."

"She wants to stay over with Rain's father."

"What's he like?"

"An asshole."

"Ah."

He looks at me, miserable. The kids are sitting on the grass. I walk over to them. It's starting to get dark.

"Okay, Augusta," I tell her, "go with them. I want you to go to school tomorrow. Call me tomorrow from school."

But as I say it, I know, we both know, I have given up. I'm letting her go.

"I will!" she tells me, jumping up.

"Don't worry. I'll take care of her," says her turbaned guru friend.

I look at Sylvan like I want to curse him. "What are you doing with these kids?" I ask him.

He just looks at me. He's really useless.

"Thank you," I say to Roy. Then I turn away and start walking down the road toward home. It seems to be getting darker by the second, and I hear big sobs coming out of me.

97

Enormous sobs. It's a cry I recognize because it is the crying of nightmares. The sobs are from deep within me and they hurt and they get louder as I approach my house, which stands so white and silent in the springtime night.

I go to the phone and call my parents. "She's gone," I tell them, and they can hardly understand me because I am crying so hard.

"Augusta's gone," I say. "I let her go."

The lamplight in the kitchen's beautiful. I have a big, gold-colored ball around the lightbulb. It's been there for years. Since right after Ben moved out. It makes the kitchen seem so warm and wonderful. I remember it was a real bitch to hang. But I managed it in that dogged energy of postdivorce, when I was fixing things that had gone unfixed for years. Suddenly ripping the linoleum right off the old wooden counters. Slapping paint up on the walls, obscuring the drab wallpaper with taupe eagles, inherited along with the shaky pipes and faulty wiring that had adorned our marriage. That was a time of energy and vision. I was amazed at all that I could do. The children were so little then and thought that I was wonderful. I called them down, in the near evening, from their rooms when I had finally hung the light above the table in our little kitchen. I'd painted all the woodwork glossy white. The golden globe shone serenely on the tall old cabinets.

"Ah!" said Augusta, looking up at it. I was still standing on the chair from which I'd hung it, arms aching from being raised so long.

"It looks like the sun!" she said. "You did it, Mommy!"

I miss her so.

10

AFTER THE TERRIBLE NIGHt with Augusta, I finally called the "education consultant" that a friend had recommended. My friend described a society I never knew existed. Schools for troubled children. Kids in gangs. Wilderness programs where they yell in your face and put you on the desert with a stick. "Escorts" who take children when the parents can no longer manage, take them on airplanes to places out west where people work with them. Group homes. Lockups. Emotional growth. It doesn't matter if the children don't want to go.

"It's a last resort," she told me.

At the time she was considering a program for her own daughter. But then her own daughter wound up moving away to live with her father. That's something they do, too, the divorced mothers who have raised the children. When the children get too hard, they send them to their fathers. And the fathers, at first, are delighted. Their daughters! Their sons! At last! Not just for the weekend, not just for a week in summer, but for always—with all their things! Their stereos, their clothes, their castanets. And the kids are delighted because the kids are so sick of their mothers with their mothers' rules and their mothers' sad faces and their mothers' curfews and their mothers' disappointment. And everybody's happy—for a time.

And then the fathers find out that the children are smoking dope in the bathroom. That's the first thing. And then they get a call from the school that the children were not in school, even though the fathers saw them get on the bus. And then the fathers smell smoke on their children's jackets, and the children deny that they've been smoking, but the fathers are suspicious and begin to believe that maybe the mothers—their ex-wives, the mothers who have seemed like tyrants—maybe weren't so bad. Maybe might have been right about the children. And then some of the liquor's missing. And then maybe some money's missing and then the mothers and the fathers, long divorced and not particularly cordial, find themselves long distance on the telephone astounded, sad, bewildered—and that's when, if they are lucky, they get ahold of the education consultants and they get a good one. And they spend the money because suddenly, though they can't really afford to, they can't afford not to do something. Quick.

So I went into the office the day after I let Augusta go and called a woman in Idaho who my friend had told me "seemed like the best of the lot."

And she told me what she does. And she told me what it would cost.

And she told me how it works.

First I send her a complete biography and a packet of school and medical and psychological records of my daughter. Also some pictures, a sort of pictorial and written time line of her life. With it I would send $1,000.

I would also need to get Ben into the ring and would get his permission to proceed.

I would also tell her what we could afford. What *I* could afford—$2,000 a month? $4,000 a month? $5,000 a month?

"It can go all the way up to a hundred thousand a year, but I don't think you need that," she told me.

Her voice was soothing. She was used to mothers like me. I had told her everything in a rush. Had described the scene from the night before, and had told her what I was afraid of, told her how scared I was. None of it shocked her.

I went ahead and did it. Sent the money. Sent the photographs of Augusta at different ages. I took them out of the photo albums. A picture of pretty Augusta as a baby. A picture of Augusta on the ferry, sitting with Jack and me with my arms around them. A picture of Augusta with Jack on top of Mount Kineo at Moosehead Lake, that summer that we rented a shabby little cabin with a screened porch for a week. Went on a rainy canoe ride. Rented a motorboat, which none of us had ever used before. Went up the river. Picture of Augusta in her rat suit for *Charlotte's Web,* the school play, when she was so good and I went to every performance every night and waited for her special little dance. Picture of Augusta reading on the dock at Islesford, looking up and right into the camera. Picture of Augusta smiling. Picture of Augusta standing by a tree, looking off somewhere else. Picture of Augusta not looking at the camera, not looking at me. Not with Jack. Her school records. And then my own memories of her—her life, her trail through school, summers, her beginning transgressions. That I knew about. That I guessed about. The beginnings of trouble at school.

Classic case it seems to me now, seemed to me even then. "Look for changes in your children, changes in their appetite," they warn you. Closed doors. Doing poorly in school. Different friends. Long times alone. Sudden outbursts. Signs of depression. Signs of drug use. Signs of eating disorders. Signs of incipient alcoholism. Signs of sex. Signs of stealing. Signs that are difficult to read as you fly past them driving much too fast on your own highway. I think it said back there! Turn there! I'll catch the next one.

I sent it all to the consultant in a large, unwieldy packet.

Two days later she was back to me. Evening. Kids in their rooms. Augusta, home again, back to her regular routine. Up in her room, "doing homework." I check for listeners and call the consultant back.

She suggests a wilderness program for the summer. One that could start as soon as possible after school gets out—$7,000. A six-week course. It would strip away maybe—the term she used—Augusta's symptoms. Get her healthier, get her away from here. Also it would serve as an evaluation period. And then what? Maybe a school. Depending, always depending, on how much you are willing to spend.

There are schools. There are schools here. There are other schools, in Jamaica, and in Europe, and in Samoa. You can put them there. And there are smaller places. There are places in people's homes, or on their farms and ranches. In Montana. Out in Idaho. In Oregon. In western Utah. Homes with people who have worked in the field. In the field, where the bad kids go. There are programs. They are restrictive. Some of the kids go to the public schools. They can participate, but they are supervised. The people watch them. They do what we didn't do, I think. They do what I can't do.

It means, all of it means, sending her away.

The education consultant gives me the names of some

parents to call, parents who have been through this. Parents who sound, when I call them, like people I might know. Jewish. Smart. Kind. Funny. People I might be friends with, who might come up in summer and we'd hike together. People who might have children who could be my children's friends. And will be. Only not in our house. In the wilderness. In dorms. In trouble.

So I have to think about all this, but I already know. I already know she's going. Only how?

There's some money in a college account, and I can use that for the wilderness and then figure out where to get the rest of it after she's there. After she's out of the house. After I can think again.

My parents say they'll give me some money. My sister never even asks, just sends $5,000 right away. "There's more," she tells me in a letter. "We want to help."

I have to talk Ben into it. He still doesn't get how bad it is.

We have conference calls with the consultant. Ben and I have discussions that are difficult and sad. It's all my fault, I keep thinking. I want it to be his fault but it's mine.

This is all happening pretty fast. I'm barely working. I'm doing my job, but I'm doing it with half my mind.

Meanwhile everything keeps happening with the kids. Augusta gets suspended for smoking at school. "I didn't smoke," she tells me. "Everybody smokes there, anyway," she says. "They were looking for a reason."

She gets in-house suspension but then swears at the teacher and walks out of class, so then she can't go back. Can't play in the spring concert: her sax, her special dress.

She spends a day at a new friend's. A girl she knows is sleeping on the couch in the tiny house of a couple who are both enormously fat, which makes me feel oddly safe. The girl works at a lunch counter. The boy does construction.

They're both through school, barely. Both nineteen. Augusta says they're nice. "They look after me," she tells me. "We had tacos."

She comes home with her long hair dyed bright blond.

She has been threatening for years to dye her hair. I've told her no.

At first I can't tell what it looks like. I can't tell what color it is when I first come in from the glare outside.

"How do you like it?" she asks me.

I take her by the shoulder to the window and look at my daughter's hair.

She has always had such beautiful hair. The kind I longed for—straight, thick, shiny, perfect hair. A sort of beigey-golden, honey-colored, streaked-in-summer, perfect young-girl hair.

Now it's the color of the women in Wal-Mart. Now it's a bright plastic shiny brittle blond. Her skin looks wrong-colored beside it.

"What do you think?" she asks me. She is doing the thing where she's excited and happy and if I'm not happy she's furious and sad and it's my fault and it's her hair and I'm never happy and she can't be like me and I'm too tired and I'm too beat to enter that so I say, "It's okay," but even that isn't enough and she looks at me with the beginning of a glare, with the beginning of the trampling stampede of accusations, but I am smiling so wanly without reproach without really anything and something—pity?—stops her and she only smiles in a glassy glossy way.

"I'm going to Dusty's. I'll be home by midnight, don't worry. I'm meeting him downtown."

"We need to talk," I tell her, and we sit at the kitchen table in the wonderful light of the afternoon and I try not to look at her hair and we talk about her going back to school.

She gets it but she doesn't get it that she's been suspended. She thinks she can still be in the concert. Thinks she can still do everything, just not go to class.

There's a little snag when she sees she won't be in the concert. With her new hair. With her shiny sax. With her new dress. But that's her other life. And she has left it. Her new life is full of people I don't know, full of people in the parking lots hanging around, people who drive around, people who get the kind of jobs that kids get in the summer and then keep having all their lives while their teeth go bad and their drinking accelerates and they skirmish with the law, get beat up by their husbands, take on debt, find young kids to get stoned with because the young kids think they're cool—these are her new friends. And they wouldn't have gone to the concert anyway, the prissy spring concert at the high school. So it doesn't matter anyway, she says.

"I'll take you downtown," I tell her. "You can drive."

She's got her permit. She is going to get her license any day now.

She can barely drive. She doesn't pay attention. Wants to play the radio instead and change the stations. Wants to open the windows and feel her new hair blowing all around her face. Wants to drive fast with her sunglasses. Wants to wave to other people. Wants to imagine herself driving. Wants to drive, but doesn't want to ever steer the car.

We get downtown. He's waiting for her, Dusty, in his truck with another lumbering boy in too-big pants.

I haven't known what to expect of this Dusty that I've heard so much of. "He's bad," Bill's told me in a low sad voice. "He's no good." So I want to get a look at him and see for myself if he is really bad.

He swings out of his truck as our car pulls up and noses into the sidewalk.

We get out and stand on the sidewalk, wait for him. He's shorter than I had expected, looks less like a lowlife and more like a preppy in his expensive sailor's jacket and his short, neat hair. But it's his eyes, I see. His eyes are evil.

He's seventeen! I think later to myself. How can he be already evil? But he is. He's evil. Standing on the sidewalk near him, with my daughter, in the light spring air of late afternoon on the sunny street, that's what I think. I think evil. I get a little chill then like an evil chill. I get a chill and I look into his eyes and there's nothing there. They're dark eyes and he speaks with a hoarse voice and he's polite, oh yes. Very polite and calls me by my name and even shakes my hand but he's a bad boy. I can feel that. And if it weren't for the education consultant and for the packet that I have sent out to her, if it weren't for the deposit I've already sent locking in a place for Augusta, I'd be grabbing Augusta by her arm and tugging her back into our car into our nice car. I'd drive her home and shove her in the house. My girl. My girl, so little in her overalls with her hair and with her darling eyes. In spite of what she'd yell at me. In spite of how she'd hate me and she'd yell. But I am so afraid she'll run away and then all of it—the plan, the promised salvation, the money—all of it will just be down the drain. So I just give him a look, this evil boy, a look that I hope will scare him and shut him up and keep him off her. I tell him *"Ten"* and get into my car.

And I go home.

Everything seems to go much quicker now. All of a sudden it's all decided. I'm sending her away. I don't know if it's the right thing. I don't know what to do. At least I'm doing something.

I go to see the woman in Bangor again.

I tell her what's been going on. She listens. I cry and she watches me.

"Here's what I can do," I tell her. "I can just let it go on the way it's going, and hope that it gets better. I can send her away to one of these schools or camps or something. I can put her in a hospital. I can let her go to jail."

"It's like breast cancer," she tells me. "It's a terrible situation. There's no good solution. But I can tell you this. This is not normal adolescent behavior. This is extreme. She is endangering herself. She is putting herself at risk for rape. She is putting herself at risk for AIDS. She is putting herself at risk for being beat up. For an OD on drugs. For an arrest. For a car accident.

"You can't fix this. You are not helping her. She won't let you help her. She hates you too much right now. And you can either let her go and wait until she hits rock bottom or you can intervene. But there's no easy answer and nothing's going to make you feel good."

"But what if I let her 'hit rock bottom' and she dies?"

"That's possible," she says. "That's one of the chances you'd take."

I already know. I already know I'm sending her to Idaho to the wilderness thing. The cost alone gives me some comfort. And the other parents, parents who have done this, have told me it was the best thing they ever did. "I saved her life," they tell me. "I saved his life," they say over the phone. They all say that. And they all say also, "I have no doubt." And they all remember how hard it was to put their child out of their house. Some of them took them away themselves. Some of them hired the escorts. But all of them say that they are glad they did it. And all of them say they have no doubt.

On the drive home I think about what the woman in Ban-

107

gor has said to me. I keep thinking about breast cancer. I keep thinking about rock bottom. I keep thinking about risk. And I know I've already decided.

So I have to get through the next few weeks. That's all. Keep her alive for the next few weeks before we can get her out there. Ben has agreed to it. He is reluctant but he has agreed to it. He will take her out. Because neither of us can stomach the idea of an escort.

There is one in particular the parents use. The consultant has told me about him. He's black. He's six foot eight. He travels with a woman who is small and blond and very very strong. You pay them a whole lot and they come early in the morning. "It's best if you set it up and have the kids at home, but even if you don't, they find the kids. They've done this before."

They've done this all over America. In the predawn dusty light parked silently in front of silent houses, met at the door by frightened parents, they go into the children's rooms, the rooms the parents have been forbidden to enter. The children are asleep. The parents wake them. They wake them remembering all the times they have awakened their children in this room, all the times they have touched their wonderful hair and stroked their heads and said, "It's time to wake up, honey." All the times before this time.

And the parents say, as they were instructed to say: "This is Will. He's taking you with him on a trip. He's taking you to a program you're enrolled in."

That's part of it—the disorientation.

The kids wake up, startled, too sleepy yet to be grumpy or in the costume of their hatred and their cool. They stare around just the way they used to stare around, big lipped with sleep, their hair all mussy. "What?"

The parents repeat themselves. And then they say what they've been told to say while all the time looking at their children's sleepy faces thinking I can't do this I can't do this. This is my child. I can't do this. They say what they have practiced saying: "I love you. But I can't keep you safe anymore. I have to do this. I love you." And they leave the room. And they go out crying, and they go down the hall or they go into another room, or they go downstairs and stand in the living room, lean against a wall, and because it is so early in the morning, even though it is summertime, the wall feels curiously cool and they notice this, the coolness, against their backs as they listen, trying not to listen, but listening to their children asking questions and the big man answering.

The voices of the children accelerate as they figure out what's going on and they become louder and harsher and more familiar. This is the anger. This is the fury they have listened to and this is why, they tell themselves, they are doing this thing that feels, because of the earliness of the hour, and because of the terrible chill of the wall behind them, and because of the dusty light and the silent street and their child's bewilderment—this thing that feels like a crime.

And then, as they have been told it would happen, the children are dressed and led away down the stairs. And though they have been told not to look around at them the parents can't help but look around at them as the children are led down by the tall man and the little woman with the blond hair who's supposed to be so strong.

The parents are relieved to see that the children are not being restrained, just led, but when the children see their parents they shout with rage and they are screaming, swearing, and crying out loud as they are led away through the kitchen out the door to the waiting car.

This is the way it can happen, but we have agreed that we will not do this. Ben has said he will take her when the time comes, out to Idaho, out to camp.

II

Memorial Day weekend goes by in a dream. Sometimes Maine is perfect on Memorial Day weekend, except
for the blackflies, but here along the coast, the blackflies
aren't so bad. I climb a lot of mountains. The mountains on
this island are very little. You can climb one in an hour and a
half: trail, rock, tree, open ledge, view of the sea, back down
and loop around the wet sweet springtime wood.

Ben has taken Augusta to Boston for the weekend. The
house relaxes. I had no idea how much tension was in
the house until Augusta was gone. No big music banging in
her room. No smell of smoke wafting out from under her
door in spite of the old clothes she's stuffed under there like
rags. No scurrying footsteps in the center of the night. No
worrying if she will come, she won't come home, if I'll have
to get up out of bed and go out into the night again looking
for her.

Jack and I creep about the house like two old men.

He has his little ways. I have mine. We know each other.

We talk very quietly. The house is quiet. Nobody's yelling at anybody else. Nobody's furious not talking in their rooms. Nobody's on the telephone saying fuck this, fuck that, fuck you, fuck you, fuck you, my fuckin' mother. Nobody's standing in the doorway just outside the room—whatever room, whatever room I'm in—and slouching on one hip; nobody's sneering at me, saying, "What are you going to do about it?"

Nobody's making me sad. Nobody's making me mad. Nobody's making me feel inadequate, helpless, hopeless, lost. Nobody's here.

And I could see how it could be, if she weren't here.

I see that I could maybe get up in the morning and just get dressed.

I could go out for a walk and not think: What's happening at home? What is she doing?

I could make a meal and nobody would be there not eating it with me. Nobody would sit down and stare malevolently at me over the food and then stomp out and leave me angrily, sadly staring at the food.

I could have a conversation with my son.

I could have my boyfriend over and nobody would be there to remind me that she hated him. That he is terrible. That he is mean.

I could read a book.

I could sit on the porch.

I could talk on the phone.

I could go out, go in, go up the stairs, go down, and I'd be safe.

If Augusta were not here.

But she's my daughter.

✿

Ben calls me from Boston: "She's being really great on this trip. Maybe we're being too hasty, sending her away."

"It's all set, Ben."

In the evening Jack makes hamburgers on the grill and we eat them at the kitchen table off paper plates. It stays light so late. The air is like velvet. On Sunday we sleep late and then wander around the house luxuriously barefoot. The grass is green in the yard and in another week the lilacs will be in bloom. The lilacs always bloom on Augusta's birthday. I used to always put a big bouquet for her on the table in the morning. When we first lived here, when we were married, Ben picked lilacs and put them all over the house for me when I got back from the hospital with my new daughter.

Monday. Memorial Day. There's a parade through town every year—the school bands—the elementary school and the high school in their outfits with the great big drum. Augusta has been in the parade every year since about fourth grade, when she started playing the sax. They had a wonderful music teacher. They played marches. They played "Louie Louie." They played "Wooly Bully." The town came out. And there were speeches on the pier. It felt like an old-fashioned time and I, ragged ex-peacenik, Vietnam protester, never missed a year. The families of our town spread out on the lawn by the harbor with the younger kids for the patriotic speeches and the prayers. But this year neither of my children would be in the parade and so, when my son went down on his bicycle to watch, I said I wasn't going. He was surprised, but then he went away.

Instead I took a hard hike fast up two little mountains

near Southwest. Fists clenched part of the way. Ready for the fray. Ready for what comes next.

✿

They arrive at three. I'm sitting on the porch. I hear them drive up, but I can't see them because the house faces the other way. Augusta comes through the house, looks out at me through the screen door.

"Hi Ma," she tells me, goes upstairs, and I can hear her in my room right away calling a friend to come and get her.

Ben lopes around the side of the house.

"We need to talk," I tell him.

"She wants to see her friends," he says.

"Listen," I tell him. "We need to talk. Did you talk to her?"

"Did I tell her?"

"Not just that. Did you talk to her? She was missing overnight before you took her. She hasn't been to school in almost a week. Did you talk about any of that?"

"We talked. We had a really good time."

"But did you talk about what she needs to do?"

"She doesn't want to go back to school. She says it's stupid. She wants to go to that place in Camden. Get her GED. She wants to take some time off. I suggested maybe she could go to Italy. She could do art there."

"Are you kidding? Go to Italy? What's she going to do there? Don't you get it? She's taking drugs. She's out of control. She's dropped out of school. She needs help. There's something wrong."

"Well. She says she just needs to have more freedom. That you control her too much."

Whose side is he on now? This makes me crazy. I go into

the house. I go upstairs. She's in my room. Bright blond false hair. New clothes her father bought her. She'd gone away without clothes, so he bought her new ones. Bright cheap shirt. Big bell-bottoms. She's tiny. She's beautiful but she looks like someone else's daughter now. She turns around at me, doesn't bother putting her hand over the receiver. "What?" impatiently.

"We need to talk," I tell her.

"I'm on the phone," she says.

"Well, get off the phone. We need to talk."

I feel taller than I've been in months. I feel so tall. "Get off the phone and come out on the porch."

"NO!" she yells, slamming down the phone and following me. "You can't just come into a room and tell somebody to get off the phone. You can't just interrupt. That's rude."

"It's my room, Augusta."

I'm enormous. Going down the stairs of my house I can't believe my head doesn't brush the ceiling. I'm gigantic with my power and my determination. All those mountains. All those prayers. With her away. The sleep.

We go out onto the porch.

"I can't believe Martha," she says to her father. "She's psycho. She made me get off the phone."

She turns to me. "Okay—*what?*" in her worst voice.

"Well, you haven't been in school. And you just took off the other night without letting us know where you were going."

"Since when is it 'us'?"

"We just want to know where you are," Ben says placatingly to her.

"Yeah, right."

"So we need to figure out some rules," I continue. "This isn't working. You're out of control and I can't live like this anymore."

"Fine. So just let me do what I want and there won't be any problems."

"No. I can't do that. You're my daughter. You're making bad choices. You're not taking care of yourself."

"Don't yell," Ben says.

"I'm not yelling. Look, you can either stay here and follow the rules or you'll have to go live with Daddy."

I can't believe these words are coming out of my mouth. Neither can she. Neither can Ben. He looks stricken.

"Now wait a minute. Don't get out of control," he tells me. And of course then I want to shoot him.

"I've *been* out of control. We've all been out of control, Ben," I tell him. "I'm taking control. I refuse to live like this anymore."

"Whatever," Augusta says, looking off down the yard like she could care.

"I'm not going back to school, anyway," she says.

"But maybe there's some other school," Ben pleads.

I can't believe this. We're all nuts. What are we—bargaining with her? That's what we've been doing! Bargaining. Oh, you don't like this? How about that? Oh, you don't want to stay in? Okay go out. You don't like school? Okay, you don't have to go. But now it's different. Now I'm tall.

"NO!" I say. "No. That's not an option. She didn't get into the Cambridge School. She made no effort to get into the Alternative School. And she can't live here unless she's going to do what she needs to do."

"I'm not living with Daddy," she says. "I don't want to live in Ellsworth."

"I'll move," he says.

I stare at him with her stare. God!

Ben says, "I'll call Robin. She wants you to do some painting for her this week. Then we can see how things go."

"I don't want to start tomorrow. I want to see Anita."

"Okay," her father says. "I'll see if you can start Wednesday."

"But I'm not going to work all day. And I'm not staying at your house."

"Yes you are, Augusta," I say, finally and firmly. "Yeah. You can stay here if you go back to school and you're in on time and you obey the rules. Otherwise you have to go to your father's."

"You can't kick her out!" Ben tells me. "You're out of control," he tells me in the way that I remember, the way that irritated me so thoroughly a hundred years ago when we were married.

"Watch me," I tell him.

Augusta's staring at me with her furious face.

I look right at her. "I love you, Augusta, and I miss you when you're not here. But I can't live like this anymore."

"Fine!" she yells. "Take me to Anita's," she instructs her father.

"All right," he says, giving me a look that says you are the bad parent I am the good parent shouldering the weary burden all alone. "I'll pick you up at eight."

"I'll call you."

They set off across the yard toward his old car, still bickering.

"Eight."

"I said I'd call you!"

"When?"

"I don't know, Ben."

By the time I hear the car start up in the driveway they're both yelling—Augusta in her wild voice and Ben, quieter but yelling too. The car starts up, backs out, drives off, and they are gone.

I find I'm shaking. But I feel exultant. Only it's a sour hollow victory over my daughter, over my old ex-husband, over my own intimidation. I'm tall, all right. But she is still my daughter.

✿

For the next few days I am busy getting ready for her trip.

She's going on her birthday, which is a week from Sunday. I think she still doesn't know.

Tuesday: nothing.

Wednesday: I hear nothing from her.

I try calling her but she won't talk to me.

Jack asks me when she's coming back from Daddy's. I say I don't know.

Luckily the days are long. I can get out and hike in the morning before I go to work, in the evening when I get home after work. I almost never have to sit still. I'm always moving.

In the evening if it's rainy, or if Jack's not there, I could do anything. I rent a movie on the way home from work. But the VCR isn't working. The little red light won't go on. I'm all set with my supper, sitting in the gold velvet chair opposite the TV, which won't show me the movie. Stays with its blue light on. I don't really feel like eating my sandwich anyway. Grilled cheese. I just sit there, looking at the blue screen.

✿

Ben and I have another long distance conference call with the education consultant. Ben makes me wild. He says he doesn't want Augusta to feel like she's no good. He wants family therapy. He wants her to go to the Wilderness Program and then come home and live (with me) and all of us go into family therapy and all of us get fixed.

I don't want Augusta to feel bad either, but I think she feels terrible right now. Having her out of the house for almost a week, I've been able to think again.

"I think she's very sad right now," I say into the phone.

Ben sighs. I know he's crying.

"I can't fix it," I say. "I'm beyond helping her or she's beyond receiving help from me."

I know I'm quoting, but I can't help it. It's the truth.

"She's not so bad," he says. "She's really a great person."

He just doesn't want anything to be the matter.

I'm the bad one. I feel like I'm stuck being the cruel hard cold mercenary mother, making the money, rushing off to work, making the decisions, imposing sentences, while he gets to be the kind gentle loving dad.

My friend Howard tells me he saw her walking in Bar Harbor down the street. "She looked sad," he tells me.

She won't talk to me when I call. I haven't seen her.

In one week she's flying out. She still doesn't know.

The rain starts. In June sometimes it rains all month. It's not too cold, but it rains and rains and you think oh God it's going to be one of those summers.

Monday night I call again. She picks up the phone by accident. "Hi Mommy," she says.

"I miss you," I tell her. I tell her I love her. She hangs up.

The next night when I'm sleeping the phone rings right next to my head. I don't know who it is at first. It's someone yelling. Some lady yelling at me. "Fuck you! Fuck you! Fuck you! Thanks a lot! Nice sixteenth birthday present for me MOMMY! I hate you! I hate you both! Fuck you!"

I hold the phone in both hands, lying in bed on my side, stare at the wallpaper, listen to my daughter yell at me.

I try for that sure voice but I got woken up and I'm disoriented, strange. My heart is pounding. "Augusta?" I say. But she's hung up.

12

SOMEHOW, all this time, I'm going to the office. I'm taking phone calls, negotiating little deals, trying to get elected to a board I want to get on. I'm meeting with people. My sales manager quits. I hire another one. A big company wants to buy the radio stations. We're in the ratings. I sign the payroll. I give speeches. I go to Rotary. I give the news. Wearing my suits. Wearing my shoes. I drive my car. I listen to the radio. When it's not raining I open up the sunroof for the first time since last fall.

But mostly it is raining. It seems like every day. Though I can usually go out in the morning for my walk. It isn't raining then.

I walk down around the shore of the town, down to the pier at Gilpatrick Cove, and stand and look down into the water. One morning the water there is like a blessing, completely still. It is early and the water is filled with pale white luminescent jellyfish like little round moons opening and closing, moving slowly through the water. Thousands of them. All of them all moving, all of them swaying, opening and closing, filling the water with light.

And on one of those June mornings, before it starts with the wind and the rain, I see my first starfish of the season, five-speared and open perfectly underwater when the tide is out. By August I will count up to a hundred starfish, standing in this one place. They are my omen.

My parents show up at my office. They want to talk. They look different now. They've gotten older. My father looks a little shrunken but the same—my same old dad. My mother just looks sad. They come into my office together, unannounced. They've driven up. I knew they were coming by their footsteps on the stairs coming up to my office. I know their tread.

They sit down opposite my desk in two chairs.

They look at me.

"Any progress?"

"Not really," I say. I try to keep my face still. I'm at my office. This is where I hide from my life. If I open just one little crack in here I'll just start crying. And once I start I'm never going to stop. So I'm mute as a stone. I'm stolid, almost stern, with them.

"Ben's told her that she's going to Wilderness."

"And is he resigned to it?" my mother asks. She has started to cry. My father reaches out and puts his hand over her hand but she barely notices.

"I don't know," I tell them. "He's doing it. He's taking her out there. Next Sunday. On her sixteenth birthday."

My mother keeps crying. My father just looks seriously at me like he's listening to an important lecture.

I wish I had something for them. Something good. I've been bringing them trouble all my life. First me and now my daughter. And my divorce. And my own sorrow bundled up, an uncomfortable burden that I carry around with me, plop down before them. It was one thing when they were younger but now they haven't the heart for it. They haven't the shoulders for it. But I keep coming.

And she doesn't even know the half of it.

She draws herself together. "You're doing the right thing, honey," my mother tells me. "I have no doubt you're doing absolutely the right thing. And she'll get through this. We all will."

It would be nice if we had something else to talk about. But this is it.

Thursday. She leaves on Sunday morning. I have sent the packet with the insurance forms, medical information, my permission, $7,000. Ben has the tickets. I'm so afraid that something will go wrong.

Thursday morning I'm up early, gritty with fatigue. On my walk I can't even taste the air or anything. I'm just doing it because that's what I do. I know the air is a certain way. I know the ocean looks a certain way because I've seen it for years, but I'm just walking fast, just moving forward.

I have a session with my regular therapist that morning. He's been through all of this with me. He hasn't been able to fix anything but there is something so reassuring about the quiet gray room in which I meet with him, the dull magazines in the waiting room: *Condé Nast Traveler, Psychology Today,* a *Reader's Digest.* Who gets these magazines? His colleague? Does he get them especially to put in here? Nondenominational, nonthreatening? Or are they the things he reads? His wife reads? I don't know. The coatrack's soothing, and the quiet chair. His room is dull and gray. Like being in a cloud. It's small and safe. Sometimes, when I come in right after someone else—a couple, maybe, whose voices I heard while I was waiting, rising and falling from behind the door—I can smell emotions in the room. Then I have to ask him to open up the window for me. I sit on the little couch and look at him and look at the photographs of his children, who all seem perfect and blond and healthy. In the pictures they are batting tennis balls, doing cartwheels across wide, sunlit lawns, standing with their arms around their parents. Two parents. Are these his credentials as a counselor? His happy family? Sometimes I imagine that they're merely props. Did he pay models? Do these people really exist? But once I saw him in a restaurant with his wife and daughter and they seemed perfectly content and at ease with one another. And no one had my surly daughter's face.

I tell him where we are.

Last March, in the midst of what I thought was the worst (I didn't know that each week would bring a new worst and the old worst would become nostalgically not so bad in retrospect and by comparison)—last March, when everything was falling down around me and I sat on this little couch and asked: What can I do? What can I do? he told me, "Get a big white car, a bottle of vodka, and just get out of town. Start driving."

My friends, who take their therapy more seriously than I, told me that that was an irresponsible thing to say. "He said that? He's your therapist?"

But I thought it was wonderful, hilarious. And later, remembering the way he said it, and the time, and what came next, I realized I should probably have done it.

123

But now we're past all that. It's not going to be me driving out of town. It'll be my daughter at the wheel of that big white car.

"It's over," he tells me now, in early June.

"You'll never go back to that time. Augusta won't live with you again, not in the same way. She won't be holed up in her room. She won't be yelling at you, furious. You and Jack are going to be all right. There's still this to get through. Getting her out there. But it's over. You've made the plan. You've got it all organized and someday she'll understand what you have done for her. How much you love her."

I feel good. The sun comes briefly out. I walk back to the office. I feel good. I feel relieved, already. It *is* over.

This has been hard for Jack. This time with Augusta with the craziness and the yelling and the nights and all of it—it's been terrible for him. Just getting through the days.

He loves his sister. They're very close. Only sixteen months apart in age, and also close in the way that siblings get when they have had to grow up going back and forth between their parents' houses. That brings kids close. They have their little jokes and secrets and their own language. I love their friendship although sometimes it excludes me and it hurts my feelings. Their secret names for me. Their rolling eyes.

It's almost the end of school. One more week. This summer Jack has a job on the ferry. Good. Next year he can go to the Alternative School. One more week.

Thursday afternoon. I'm at my desk working on some stuff I have to get done, losing myself in it.

The phone rings. Bill from the school.

"Jack's in trouble."

"What happened?"

"It seems he assaulted a teacher. He's been accused of threatening a teacher with a knife."

"A knife."

"Well, it was in cooking class. A bread knife. The teacher isn't going to leave it alone. She's insisted we call the police. You better come down, Martha."

I pull everything off my desk into my bag and go.

Driving down to the Island I'm barely breathing.

I park the car and storm into the school.

I've got my umbrella and it makes a sharp sound as I walk through the hallways of the empty school. Everyone has left. I can hear my heels on the floor. I can hear my umbrella on the floor. I feel as if the school is full of teachers but they are hiding from me in the back of the rooms. Back in the offices. Afraid of my fury, afraid of my daughter, afraid of my son.

This is the school that wins awards, that sends basketball teams to Portland. That sends jazz bands triumphant to Washington, D.C., to compete under the cherry blossoms. This is the school that wins the drama prizes. Whose parents attend the games. Whose scores are high. Whose self-congratulatory school board sits and meets and talks about the high scores the good colleges the big awards. The front hall is full of statues of brass and bronze and medals. There are banners hanging in the big wide gym that gets stuffed on winter nights with proud community members for the basketball games. A school full of teachers with new ideas. An enormous special ed section and "resource rooms" and art rooms and theater and academic excellence. But it has failed my children. And when I come here I feel horrible and lost. I am trespassing in the hallways reserved for happy parents.

Parents with normal kids who can excel here—do excel here. Win the prizes. Give the speeches. Ring the bells.

This is the school, my daughter tells me later, where you can get any drug you want anytime you want: grass, 'shrooms, LSD, cocaine, heroin, crank, crack, speed. And now, with antidepressants all the rage, they're for sale, too. They grind them up. They sell them. People take them to get high.

It's nobody's fault.

But I am furious.

All I know is, this is the school that has failed my children. First Augusta. Now Jack.

And I walk through the halls this afternoon with my umbrella making a snap-click on the floor like a soldier marching alone into the fray. The teachers look up from their conversation as I go by and I know they have been talking about the latest scandal, my son's scandal, because of the way they look at me and they stop talking. What a mother! Two kids like that! I know what they're thinking. I snap by.

I find someone in the front office.

"What's going on?" I ask her.

"Um. I don't know for sure. Jack's left. He went home. I think Bill's with the teacher. In his office."

"Who is it?"

"Lynn Karp."

I wheel around, say over my shoulder, "They better not fuck with my son."

"You don't know everything that happened," she tells me in a quiet voice.

And then I get it. It doesn't matter how angry I get. It doesn't matter if he did or didn't threaten. It doesn't matter if it's right or wrong. She's the teacher. She will win.

Bill's office.

She's sitting there.

I know her. I've never seen her before. But I recognize her. I recognize her by her frizzy hair. I recognize her by her dull slightly googly eyes. I recognize her by her long nervous fingers once beautiful. I recognize her by her stupid L.L. Bean denim jumper and her withery neck and her no-stocking legs and her cork sandals. I recognize her all right. I know her tale. She is a Fascist Hippie. Old school. She's from away. She's from the land where people all agree with one another and there are clear certain rules about what is good and what is bad. She is as rigid as the most rigid right-wing Christian nutcase but she's liberal. She is organic. She does the right things. I'm sure she disdains my radio stations. She disdains my sixty-second ads. She disdains my son with his huge pants. His big size scares her, his black talk scares her. His cap scares her. And her fear of him, and her disdain for him, has made her dangerous.

She is sitting on the chair in Bill's small office. She turns to me and looks at me with her googly eyes.

Bill, behind his desk, right away knows how mad I am. He is probably a little amused. He's seen it all. And now with these two warring women in his room, the air is thick with premenopausal confrontation. Hormone heaven. Worse in some ways than when he gets two teenage girls in here spitting like cats.

He introduces us, looking for a low-key angle.

I don't shake hands.

I already really, really hate her.

She tells me in a monotone what happened.

Jack was late to class. Jack asked to go to the bathroom. When he came back the other kids were already tearing up their bread for the topping on the casserole. I can see it. He comes back. Taller than anybody. Embarrassed. Not sure what to do.

She tells him to wash his hands. He already did. In the bathroom. I can tell her that without even asking him. He's Jack. He probably washed his hands five times!

The world is my enemy.

The world is my enemy.

The world is my enemy.

He says he's washed them. She tells him to wash them again. She goes over and stands beside him to make sure he washes them. He starts cutting up his bread with a bread knife.

She tells him to tear the bread, not to cut it.

He keeps cutting the bread. He is cutting it in big whaps like a chef he saw on a funny movie that we watched the other night. He is pretending he is that funny chef.

She doesn't know that. She sees a big boy with a big knife whapping at the bread. Bread he's supposed to be tearing, like the other children. She doesn't like him. He knows she doesn't like him. Teachers generally don't like him. He's too big. Keeps to himself.

So now she goes over and tells him, "That's not the way you use the knife."

And then, according to her, he raises the knife at her and he says, "I'll show you what I'd like to do with this knife!"

And then she makes him go down to the office, where she files a complaint. Has the police called. Gives a statement.

"I won't have him in my class," she tells me now.

I don't say anything for a moment.

Then I say, "This has been a very difficult time for my family. Jack's sister is having a really hard time right now. You may not know it, but she's left school. She's living with her father. We're sending her away. Jack's under a lot of stress. He'd never hurt anyone."

She looks at me with her googly eyes. She watches me with her dull blue eyes and she says, "My heart goes out to you as a mother, but as a teacher I have to think about the safety of my students."

"Don't do this to him," I tell her.

I tell her like a curse. I tell her, like I'm casting a bad spell on her, on her own organically fed, carefully bred little Christian children with their straw hair and their pale eyes. "Don't do this."

I tell her Jack's supposed to go to an award banquet this weekend. I tell her Jack's got a date with a senior for the prom. I tell her Jack really needs to finish out the year and that if she does this he'll be suspended for the rest of the year. I tell her. I'll do anything. I'm ready to plead, threaten, make terrible waves. I ask her again, "Please, don't do this."

But she's done it. And right now the policeman is coming down the hall.

"She has to give a statement," Bill tells me.

"Can I stay?"

"No."

So then it's the lawyers and the DA and the juvenile worker. Which is why on Friday, two days before Augusta is flying out to Idaho, I am driving to work with Jack in the car beside me. At a time when all of my attention should be on my boy, I am thinking about my girl, thinking about my job. Thinking about what's left of the tattery tatters of my life.

As we pass the round building that used to be the Cheese House, I tell Jack about the Wilderness Program. I always try to get to him first with the news, to put my own spin on it, before Augusta's rage drives it veering off in a different direction. Now I tell him a little more. She's leaving Sunday morning. Daddy's taking her.

"Do you think she wants to go?" he asks me.

"No," I tell him. "But I have to do something, you can see that, can't you, Jack? She's in danger. She's putting herself in danger. She could get in a car accident. She's taking drugs. She could get AIDS." (I don't say how she could, but we both know.)

"Is she mad?"

"Yeah. I think she probably hates me right about now. And she's probably going to hate me for a long time, but I'd rather have her hate me, Jackie, all her life, than have her dead."

It's easier to say than feel, but just saying it makes me feel tall again.

"I have to get her some things today," I tell him. "I have to go to Reny's and get her some stuff for Wilderness."

"Like what?"

"I don't know. She has to have certain things. A one-piece bathing suit. A sweatshirt. A parka."

"She won't like what you get her."

"She doesn't like anything right now. Anything I do. But I'm her mother. I don't get to quit."

We meet with a lawyer and I work in my office while Jack comes in and out, goes over to the library, downtown, comes back. In the middle of the afternoon the lawyer calls. He can't do anything. The school won't even meet with us for two weeks. So even if they unsuspend him, Jack's out for the rest of the year. He can't go to the prom. He can't go to the sports banquet. He can't go to graduation. He can't go to the Alternative School next year unless we convince them over the summer that he should.

He's not in my office right then so I get to cry.

It feels as if someone has been beating me with the flat bent blade of a snow shovel. That's all I can imagine. Someone beating me over and over, over the head, over the shoulders, over the head again, and just when I get back up a little, on my hands and knees, start to rise again, thumping me over the shoulders, on the head, with a bent gray metal-ridged shovel made for shoveling the wet thick snow of winter, beating me over and over and over and over all year.

When he comes in again I have to tell him.

He's fifteen, so he doesn't react. He knows I've done what I could do. He knows that I've been trying everything. To get him back in. To fight with the school. To convince them, bully them, shame them into letting him back. But it's no good. It makes me sad how he accepts it like he's the one.

"Let's get out of here," I tell my son. "Let's go buy stuff for Augusta."

But it isn't any better being in the store, with my big gangly darling sullen son loping beside me, spending another $150 on stuff she isn't going to like, with me asking him, "Do you think she'll like this one or do you think she'll like that one?"

He doesn't care. He's thinking prom dream. Thinking empty days. Thinking disgrace. How can he be interested in one-piece bathing suits? In navy parkas? In plain-colored T-shirts (no black, nothing too tight, nothing too transparent).

At the checkout it's more than I thought it would be and I get that frantic high-pitched feeling. "Wait a minute!" I say.

I've added it up wrong in my head. "Wait!"

There's somebody behind me in the line who shifts from one foot to another impatiently as I put back the sweater and the second pair of pants to get the price down.

I can feel I am close to a scream.

Jack knows too. He's seen this.

But he's too spent himself, so he just says, "I'll be in the car."

"Wait," I tell him, "help me carry this."

But he is gone.

The worst part is the aloneness of it. I don't want to tell my parents all of it. All my boyfriend ever says is, "I wish there was something I could do," which makes me furious because there isn't. My ex-husband is doing what he can. He tells me it's been "a little hard" with Augusta, which makes me imagine some pretty horrible scenes. I know what "a little hard" can feel like—like you swallowed a bag of glass. They're supposed to leave in two days.

I can't talk to any of my friends. They've heard enough. I feel like I've been complaining too long to them. It's boring. It's like I have this endless disease. I can always call my sister but she's busy with her own kids and I know she's sick of it too. Everybody's sick of it. I'm sick of it. How much it hurts. Sending my daughter away. How scared I am. Will it even work? What else is there? It's the same thing over and over. The same road. The same shovel.

13

I AM BECOMING old in the kind of middle-aged way I never imagined myself. It doesn't feel intolerable. I am in between. I'm like an old twig with the young green under. You peel back the bark and there it is—the slightly sticky smoothness of the wood beneath, the brightness of the green, the tender, cream-colored, dream-colored springtime promise. But I could easily become a tidy old Maine woman with my curly hair gone gray, my "slacks," my "perm," my little shoes. I'm too lean to be the thick kind with comfortable hips, wearing a fat bathrobe, so I guess I'll be the tall kind of old woman that you see, staying remarkably the same for years and years—straight backed and firmly cheerful. But old. No longer sexy. No longer young.

I think it will be a relief, to give up all the drag and pull of desire. The disappointment and the longing and the care. Already I can feel some of the urgency slipping from me as I age. It used to rule me! Rule me! It used to run my life.

I feel it slipping away—that old pull. It should be sad, but it feels like relief.

The only thing that has mattered, really mattered, with clear sharp urgency in the past few years has been my children. They're the only ones that can pull me quite this way.

But with them lately, so little of it has been a pull toward pleasure. When they were little, and even up until a year or two ago, there were these pools of sheer pleasure. Whether from pride in something they had accomplished or in delight at how they looked or how they'd grown or understood about something or just their brief, unwilling, dear affection. My daughter, as big as she was at thirteen, fourteen years old, would still sometimes clamber up into my lap and sit there, lean against me. My son would let me hug him. These things shot through me, these happy things. But more often it was pain that felt the most distinct, and sadness and regret and longing, longing for how it used to be, or how I thought, maybe, it could become someday.

At work I'm very efficient. On the phone with clients I am amiable and efficient and even sometimes funny. I smile when I talk to them. I learned that from one of my sales managers. You smile when you're talking on the phone and you sound like you're smiling and things go better. No one knows what's really going on. No one knows I've sent my daughter away into the Wilderness, where kids go who are lost.

I'm doing everything.

I'm eating. I fix myself nice meals. I wash up.

I get a lot of exercise. It helps me sleep.

I always did all this. Even in the worst of it. Though sometimes the eating part was a little tough.

I remember one time when I came back from a business trip. We'd left on bad terms—Augusta screaming at me as I left the house early in the morning to catch a 6 A.M. plane out of Bangor. I tiptoed into her room, leaned over to her. "Good-bye, honey. I love you."

"I hate you!" she'd screamed. "I hope your plane crashes!"

When I got back she had moved in with her father. I called. It was the middle of January.

"I'm not coming home," she told me on the phone. "I'm staying here."

That time would only last a week, but I didn't know that then.

After our phone conversation I put the phone down, thought mechanically, Okay, it's time for breakfast, went over to the cupboard, opened it wide enough to see the lines of bright boxed cereals. I like cold cereal. I have it with granola on top. A glass of milk to ward off my hump. White paper napkin. One round spoon. Perhaps banana. Opened the cupboard. Saw the boxes. And stood there.

When I go into my daughter's room I can't move. It's as if the room is filled with some clear Jell-O material and I am encased in it, silenced, stilled, the moment I go through the door into her shambles of possessions.

One whole wall is covered with shelves. On the top shelf, all of her stuffed animals and dolls, from the aged teddy bear that was mine when I was a child to the Cabbage Patch she never really liked, a few nude Barbies, Candy Bear, the huge pink monstrosity my in-laws gave her, the hedgehog that went through the dryer after the lice epidemic at the elementary school, and all the others—kittens, lions, bears, Vincent the Gorilla—staring down with their glass or plastic eyes. The other shelves are filled with her books. She always refused to put any of her Golden Books away, so there they are along with R. L. Stine and *Baby-Sitters Club,* Louisa May Alcott, C. S. Lewis, Barbara Kingsolver, *Marjorie Morningstar, Tully, She's Come Undone,* and the books that she read over and over: *Go Ask Alice, How I Fell, Notes from a Suicide, High & Dry.* Her jewelry, her chains, her rings are still in the plastic bag they sent back to me when she entered the Wilderness Program. No note. No "She can't have these." Just the rings in a bag and the chains and a bracelet that she used to wear. It's like she's in jail. It's like she's really gone.

One hot, still day I start to clean her room. First I take the clothes off the floor and fold them. Then I throw out the cigarette butts I find under her bed, behind the books, on the windowsill. I throw out the marijuana and the pipes and the pills. Long ago I had given up telling her to clean her room. And long ago she had given up cleaning it. She took her bureau down to the cellar and replaced it with three large baskets to hold her clothes. The baskets are heaped up and overflowing until there is just one big mound of clothing— much of it thrift store, some of it borrowed, lots of it velvet. I start on the pile full of her odd huge pants, the tiny T-shirts she fished out of the boxes of baby clothes in the attic, her father's pajama pants, enormous sweatshirts, prom dresses from the seventies, odd socks, platform shoes and ratty sneakers, run-down Birkenstocks, black railroad boots. All heaped up in toppling piles. The floor is a sea of books, CDs, candy wrappers, old test papers, poems, drawings, presents, cards, and old photographs.

I went through all of it. I cleaned it up. I didn't want to look through her desk drawers, but I looked through her desk drawers. That's where I found the letter she had written but never sent to her summer friend Bea in California.

"My mother doesn't understand anything. I hate myself. I need somebody to listen to me. I need somebody to help me. School is a joke. I can't do anything anymore. I think I'm going crazy. I feel crazy. I don't eat anymore. I guess I'm anorexic. And yesterday I took a razor and I cut my face. I cut a big old slash across my own cheek. I don't care anymore. Next time my wrists."

"What happened to your face, Augusta?" I remember her standing in the living room. I'm on the sofa, reading my mail.

"What?" she gives me a little smile. There is a secret.

"Your cheek. You've got a cut there," I tell her.

"Oh. It happened in gymnastics."

Again that little smile. In gymnastics? But how? But that's what she told me. And that was before I knew that she never told me anything but lies.

Lies and exaggerations. Stories with enough truth in them to sometimes seem like real stories. Things that never happened. Things that could have happened.

"I don't know, I just found it."

"I lent it to her. I'll get it back."

"She told me I didn't have to do it."

"She said it didn't matter. You don't have to go to the parent conference."

"Daddy can take me."

"I can stay at Alexis's. Her mother is going to be there."

"I don't feel good. I can't go to school."

And then the longer stories. The stories that involve our own history. I didn't know. I thought that if I looked at her in a certain way, if I studied her face with my face, if I looked right into her eyes, then she would have to tell me the truth. If I wasn't angry. If I didn't yell. If I was careful. That she would tell me the truth.

"Augusta. You smell like smoke. Have you been smoking?"

"No. I don't smoke. I told you. I think smoking's disgusting. I was with some kids. They smoke, but I tell them to quit. I tell them it's bad for you. I don't smoke. I told you. You never believe me."

"Augusta, I'm worried that you're taking drugs."

"I don't take drugs. I'm a Buddhist. Buddhists don't take drugs."

"I know there are drugs out there. I know other kids use them."

"I don't. I think it's dumb. I don't even drink. Everybody drinks. Jack drinks. You never think he does anything. You always think it's me. Why don't you ever ask him what he does? Why don't you ask him if he does drugs? I don't do them."

"What about that pipe I found in your room?"

"I told you. I was holding that for somebody else. It's not mine. I told them I'd hold it for them because my mother wouldn't get mad. My mother wouldn't go looking around in my room. I told them you were cool, which you used to be. Now you're just conservative. You're not the same anymore. Daddy's cooler than you are. At least he trusts me."

"I trust her," my ex-husband tells me on the phone. "If she tells me something. I trust her. I mean, I worry, too, but I asked her and she tells me the truth. She told me she tried pot. She tried it, but she doesn't use drugs. She thinks drinking is disgusting. She says you go through her things. I think you have to respect her privacy more."

But after she went away, when I went through her jungle of a room I found everything. A vodka bottle. The grass. Pills. Papers. Pipes. Like everything else she had, she always had to have lots of it. She was always like that. Not one velvet dress. Lots of them. Not one big pair of baggy pants. Lots of baggy pants. Not one big sweatshirt to wear on the evenings when she wanted to eat until her belly ached and watch television in big soft invisible clothes, wrapped in a blanket lying in the gold chair staring at the television watching the same movie over and over again. *Ferris Bueller* over again. *Sister Act* over and over. Eating and watching and wearing her huge hiding sweatshirts.

So too with the drugs, she had to have lots of them. Had to have every kind. Had to take everything. If she could have she would have smoked fifteen cigarettes at once. I know because I was like that, too.

So I made the room presentable while she was away at Wilderness, and then I left it. And I couldn't go back in and finish the job. It was good enough. I knew I had to really clear it out. But when I went back into the room to finish cleaning, I couldn't move and so I turned and went out again, closing the door behind me.

I don't want to see my boyfriend. He is so understanding. He wants to help. He wants to be gentle with me but his touch feels scratchy. His hands irritate my skin. I feel as if I will break out in a rash if I get too close to him. I can't bear to see him. I am afraid I will lose him.

I call him in the middle of the night when I can't sleep. I know he'll go right back to sleep. That's how he is. He can always sleep. I can never sleep. I get up. The bed is so hot. I push back the covers and go into the bathroom and I drink water. I drink water from my own blue cup. The other cups, the cups of the children, are still there. Augusta's is purple. Jack's is green. The water in the bathroom tastes funny but I am afraid to go downstairs where it's so dark.

I get back in my bed. The covers are cooler for being open. I call my boyfriend from the phone next to the bed. He always answers like it's an emergency. It was an emergency plenty of times, but now all the emergencies are over except the slow meaningless endless dreadful emergency of my remaining life.

"Yes!" he answers.

"I can't sleep."

"Ahhh" (so it's just that), but he knows what's under it—the size of what's beneath.

"Okay," he says. "Do you want to talk?"

"No," I tell him. He's used to me. But when will I use him up?

Later, annoyed by his endless patience and his understanding, I read some book sitting up in the bed. But I can't concentrate even on the simplest stories—engrossing murders, love conquests, terrible histories—none of it catches me.

I get calls from Wilderness every week. They tell me Augusta's doing okay. She's not resigned to being there, but she's there. They tell me she's doing what she needs to do to be there. She sends one stingy letter that they make her write. She calls once. She sounds okay but she says she hates it there.

"I can't believe you'd send me here," she says, but she doesn't sound furious. She sounds like she's having fun.

"I'm not having fun!" she tells me, but I think she is. The counselor tells me that she's quite a girl. She thinks she's coming home at the end of the six-week course.

Meanwhile I've narrowed it down to two places.

One is in Jamaica, which she'd like, the other out in central Oregon.

The Oregon one is more expensive, but I think it's better.

I talk to parents with kids at each place. I watch the videos the schools provide. I talk to the administrators. I talk to my "education consultant." I talk to Ben.

The Oregon place is expensive. Fifty thousand a year, but they'll give me a scholarship. Half price. My sister sends me money. My parents give me money, sitting in my office, soberly writing out a check. I ransack the mutual fund with savings for college. There might not be college. There definitely won't be college if we don't do this. We're saving her life. I don't want her to be gone, but it's better with her gone. I feel so sad but it's better.

I plan to go out just before the Wilderness thing gets over. I'll go out to Oregon and look at the school, then I'll double back to Boise and meet Ben and Augusta at the "End of Trail." They have some sort of a ceremony with the kids and parents. Some of the kids go home then. Some of the kids go back into Wilderness. Some of the kids go to these different schools.

There are lots of these places. There are big schools run by big corporations for kids whose parents can't control them. Some of the people who work in these places get married and start their own smaller places built on the same ideas as the bigger places where they worked. Some are on ranches and the kids help with the ranch, and some are only for girls, some for boys and girls, and some with programs for the parents, too, and the kids who go to Wilderness go on to all these different schools. There are some that medicate the children; some that are like jails; some that are run like military camps; but in all the videos and in all the pictures everybody's smiling. The kids look rich and happy. The kids are backpacking and working. All these troubled kids are transformed into healthy smiling nice kids and at the end of each of the videos they hug their parents if their parents are there or look into the camera if the parents might watch the video and they say, "I love you Mom, I love you Dad, thank you." And the parents see the videos and look at the pictures and they think thank God thank God.

I choose the Oregon school. I get my tickets and I make my reservations. I'll need a car. I'll need some money. It is very hot.

July 1998. It's very hot.

When I look at the weather map in the back of the *Bangor Daily News* the color is yellow right across the country. Where I'm going. Where Augusta is. Hot yellow, bright.

The counselor calls. She got some spider bites. Don't worry. She got some pretty bad bites from a kind of poison spider that lives on the desert. On her face. It looks bad, but we took her to the doctor.

I think it will heal, the counselor tells me. Don't worry.

14

ONE HOT MORNING in late July I get on a plane for Oregon. I'm taking just one bag. A small bag with white clothes in it: white T-shirts, sneakers, shorts, white underwear. I want to reflect away as much of the heat as possible.

When I arrive I get a sporty (cheesy, Augusta would say) little red car from the car rental, drive past scrub bushes and twisty Western pines under the Western sky to a flat town built of gas stations and convenience stores and low flat buildings. In a shopping center there's my Best Western, where I'm staying.

My room is on the long strip of rooms. It comes with a continental breakfast in the lobby. It's really hot but there's air-conditioning in my room and I blast it, so that later, coming back after a walk across the parking lot, my room's too cold and I have to turn it off.

I eat alone at Shari's. Which has about ten kinds of pie and a very friendly waitress. It feels like the middle of the night but it's light out here for ages still. I have fajitas and ice water. I don't want to spend much money. This whole trip's expensive; the school itself.

After supper I walk back and forth across the parking lot. In the big supermarket I buy cherries and watermelon cut in chunks and a couple of tiny bottles of white wine and bring them back and put them in the little refrigerator in my room so I can have a snack later.

I have a phone card, but it's too late back home to call anyone. So I get in bed, take a Tylenol PM, turn the TV on, and watch from bed, flipping from channel to channel, watching snippets, waiting for something that will look like something that I want to watch, but it's all the same. It's all either people singing or people telling jokes or old movies or new movies or dramas with men with guns or comedies where women come into the room and do a double take or shows about teenagers who all have very clean hair and all live in nice houses in places where it is never too hot or too cold or too sad.

And the audience goes ooooooohhhhhh and laughs and laughs and laughs, like they all know these people, like they're all old friends.

In the morning it's not too hot yet when I go out across the parking lot in my shorts and T-shirt to get a jumbo coffee at the Burger King. Nobody's in there but the workers. The woman who waits on me has a black eye and Band-Aids on seven of her fingers and I think immediately her husband beat her up and worry about her lousy life out here in Dalton, Oregon, as I walk back to my room in the new light of the summer morning.

The coffee is hot and there's lots of it and I drink it sitting at the little table in my room staring right into the big mirror that is staring back at me. I write in my journal and think about my whole life, not just this odd little piece of it. There is something freeing and disembodying about being way out here in this odd desert terrain with its ring of mountains all around. The Cascades. Sisters. Brothers. Whatever. Being out here at the Best Western where I'll probably never again stay in my life only what if this does become the place where my daughter is saved and I wind up coming out here every three months for two years? Get to know the lady at the Burger King? Will she confide in me about her husband? And will I talk with her and give her the courage to leave him finally? Will I become acquainted with the tall waitress at Shari's? Get to know the streets of Bend?

What if this becomes my new life? My job, my house, my car all suddenly seem tiny. From over here, across the country, my friendships, worries, decisions seem viewed through the wrong end of a telescope. All faraway and unreal like the movie I watched soundless on the screen above as I was flying over this land.

So now, in my Best Western bland hotel room preparing for my visit to the school that is to be my daughter's school, I feel strong, full of bravery and black coffee, full of plans.

The drive over to Lyle and beyond is longer than they warned me. I pass through long stretches of dry farmland. Cows and irrigation systems, low flat houses, open, scalding sky. I've got the air conditioner ranting and the radio on but I don't know the stations out here so I scan aimlessly until I come upon the weird hip Oregon Public Radio, where my sister used to work long ago.

Lyle looks like a town that might house a prison. The

streets shuffle off to either side in uninteresting strips peo-
pled with low houses. There is a shopping center, a couple of
dingy restaurants with dusty parking lots, one fine tall old-
fashioned town-hall kind of building, a little park. I try to
think how this will seem to me if it becomes a familiar town.
Then on through the Estacada National Forest, past the long
lake with its hot glare in the morning light, along the endless
road. The air is different out here and the sides of the road
are different and it's a long long way to the small wooden sign
with the name of the school on it and the cluster of neat log
cabins and the lodge with tall wooden steps leading up that
all look smaller than the picture in the brochure they sent.

I pull in.

Rebecca Mintz, whom I've talked to on the phone, is the
admissions director and one of the founding mothers of Forest Ridge. She is smaller than I expected, but just as warm
and smart. I think she's like me. And in another life, in another time, I think we could be friends. She's smart and
forty-five and Jewish and she has her own crazy history,
which she hints at in our conversations.

"Oh yes, I was wild," she says with a laugh and I laugh,
too, relieved that I can like her and the school, that I can
send my daughter here.

Everybody seems nice, in that folksy hippie Oregon
woodsy way but with a touch of businesslike determination.
The buildings are neat and inviting. In the main lodge
there's a big room with a beautiful rug and great big pillows
where you take your shoes off, where you can have "group"
and "work on your stuff," and a long dining hall where Rebecca puts me with some girls who all look clean and nice
and neat and all are curious about my daughter: When's she
getting here? What did she do? They tell me a little bit about
themselves. *No, they didn't like it here at first. Yes, they need to*

be here. They tell me they're from California, New Mexico, outside Chicago. They got in trouble, they say vaguely, and their parents sent them here. They've been here two months, seven months, a year. They went to Wilderness. It's okay, they tell me. I try to see if they have something else to say, something that they're not saying, but I can't read their eyes. I just don't know. But they do seem like girls that my girl could be friends with. She's always had friends.

A tall man who smiles too much and has no hair takes me around to the dorm cabins. Four to a cabin. The cabins are neat. They have inspection, they have to clean them every Saturday. "We don't let them have too much stuff," my guide tells me. They allow the picture of their family on the bulletin board above the bed. A drawing. A comforter from home, a couple of stuffed animals. A few books. Everything is quiet.

These places—Forest Ridge, I'm sure the Clean Teen places, all of them—are built by people with good ideas and good intentions. They found them on certain principles and they build them up with great lofty ideals and they probably do some good. But then the original people get tired, get sick of the kids, the parents, the crises, the late nights and the broken weekends, sick of driving around at 3 A.M. looking for runaways on the lost lunar strip of Lyle, sick of the Estacada woods. And their marriages falter, and they drink too much, and they have affairs—I'm sure they have affairs with other staff—because they get close in that way you get close to people you're in battle with day after day. And just when you start to get somewhere with some kid—one of the kids that will make it—that kid runs away or gets pulled.

147

And you know a lot of these kids just aren't going to make it. It's too late. They've veered too far off. And you know it and the parents know it but you're their last best hope, because the kid has already been kicked out of half a dozen schools, has gotten kicked out of even his own public high school, has been kicked out, has run away, has taken more drugs than even you in your own heyday. This is their last chance and they have chosen this school because it sounds the best, and it costs the most, and the video was so beautifully produced and features the happy faces of the kids smiling at graduation, hugging their parents—being okay.

You have to believe in yourself and you say to them yes, I think we can work with your daughter, your son, and you take their check even though you know they don't have this kind of money. You take their money and you take their faith and you take their child and you hope that maybe you can help them.

And seven months later one big boy is hanging from a tree in the Estacada woods with a noose around his neck.

And four months later two girls are partying hearty on the streets of San Francisco with a man named Ashtray, eating handouts from good-natured citizens who feed the street kids, keep them on the street.

And eleven months later you are on the phone with the same parents and you are telling them, "We looked, but they were already a long way down the road by then. Oh yes, we've reported it. They're on the system. Don't worry."

Don't worry.

And you're telling them to "sit tight" and you're telling them to "stay by the phone" and you're telling them to pray.

They've paid so they won't have to pray, because prayer alone won't do it and you know that, too.

And now they are angry and they are sad and you feel as if

maybe they're right maybe it is your fault but you're sick of them too these rich parents with their spoiled kids. They've botched the job and handed over their botched blotched stoned kids, handed them over to you and what are you supposed to do with them? Save them? Reform them? Transform them? Undo fifteen years of craziness, of divorced yelling, bad gene pools, in six months? So what if they're paying $4,500 a month? There are no guarantees.

The next day I drive down into the mountains and think about taking a hike but I don't know the trails here and after I have parked my car on the side of the road and followed the broad path up into the forest a little ways I realize I could get killed in here. There could be bears. It's Oregon. There could be cougars. And nobody would know. It's beautiful in this different, alien forest and I promise myself that I'll come back and hike someday but not today. Instead I drive the long way back into Bend through the mountains, past the golf resorts and the condos and the mountain ski resorts, past the stretches of manufactured green on the long smooth Western highway, and I am surprised as I drive that I suddenly start to cry. I drive crying with my mouth open, staring at the road, sobbing and yelling for my daughter who is doomed to this.

That afternoon I fly to Boise, where the next day I will see my daughter at Trail's End.

In Boise I'm staying in a great big hotel. It's already late by the time I get there. I get a little table in the restaurant and order fajitas, which are the official meal of this trip, I guess, and a glass of red wine. I sit alone and eat and I'm so tired I don't even read. From my little table I watch a group of kids who are on some other sort of program ordering big plates of spaghetti, which is somehow hilarious and causes great swells of merriment when it arrives. The couple at the next small table is arguing. The man is older, alcoholic, ruined, once handsome. She's dark and round, younger and impatient. They're married to other people. This is their rendezvous in Boise.

The man lights up a cigarette and the woman asks for a second glass of wine. "A Chablis," she tells the waitress in a special voice, as if this were a fancy restaurant and this were a fancy affair and not some seedy sad one, which I think it is.

And the whole time, in the back of my mind, I'm thinking: How can I do this? How did my life get like this? How did my daughter get like this? How did I let it go?

"You let it go on too long," my father told me once, during the summer.

But I don't know. Should I have sent her here a year ago? At the first signs? Wasn't that too soon? But maybe we could have avoided that whole crazy stretch of dark road, yelling at each other, locked in battle. Everything feels wrong now and too sad. I want to concentrate on the couple with their drab illicit affair, the kids with their spaghetti and hilarity. Think about my room: how nice it is, really, for only $48 a night. I'll watch TV, I think to myself. I can watch some shows.

And tomorrow is the day I'll see my girl.

I've never been away from her this long. Never. Not ever. Six weeks and, counting the two weeks she spent at Ben's, it comes to eight weeks—two months without my daughter.

How did it get like this?

It's too sad if I go down that direction, so I double back, finish up my gluey, cold fajita, go back to my little room, and go to bed.

15

THE NEXT MORNING we all meet in the conference room they've rented for us. The Wilderness Program is associated with Forest Ridge, so Rebecca Mintz is here in her little linen dress. Ben's here. We smile ruefully at each other, sit apart. The other parents are here. These are the parents of the Wilderness children. We introduce ourselves. They are mostly couples, middle aged, the men in jeans and golf shirts, the women in floppy pants. Nobody's fancy here. It's much too hot. We talk about that—how it's supposed to get up to 104 today, 110.

"I didn't know it got like that in Boise," someone says.

I never knew anything about Boise. Never thought about Boise until this summer, when suddenly it feels like the center.

We have a lot of time together. We become almost friends—these pairs of parents who will never see one another again, who are all now part of the machinery of programs for troubled teenagers.

The kids are late. The van has broken down in the heat. They'll be here soon. Rebecca explains that they want to stop and shower before they see us. She seems so earnest and cheerful and efficient that I believe everything will be all right. It's so cold in the room with the air-conditioning that it's hard to believe how hot it is just outside the door.

Rebecca has us say our names and something about ourselves and something about our children. I will find out later, as I get deeper into this world of programs and psychology and group stuff, that this is what you always do. That's how you begin. You stand up. You say your name. You say where you are from or else the leaders prompt you, "And where are you from?" or if they remember they say, "And Martha is from Maine, aren't you?" And if you are divorced, if you are the only ones in the room who are divorced, you both have to go. And you might refer to each other as "Augusta's father" or, jauntily, "my ex," but no one does that much. We are all kinder here to one another, even our ex-spouses, than we ever have been in the world. We are all so sad about our children that here, among the other failure parents, there are no comparisons about whose kid is worse, whose kid is somehow better. It's sweetly noncompetitive. We're sympathetic. We exchange stories, but not like trophies. We exchange our stories gently and when other people speak we sometimes nod our heads. Yes. That's the way it was. Exactly the way it was. Almost the way it was.

We take turns going up and down the rows. There aren't so many of us, after all, the parents of eleven children. A few grandparents looking a little out of place. The one black lady from Chicago. Rebecca bustles us along. We can have coffee or cold drinks.

Then there's a little buzz after the long wait. They're coming! They're coming! The van is in!

They come in through the big doors one by one, cleaned up, sunburnt, healthy, normal-looking kids, nice-looking kids. Kids with good teeth and good hair and good genes. Kids who have had plenty of fluoride and orthodontia and regular checkups. They go over to their parents. (All but the little fat boy, whose mother isn't coming, whose mother is in Europe, who is going back to Wilderness for round two.)

But where's Augusta? Where is my daughter?

She is the last one to come in. She is wearing the dress we bought together last spring. Green. Too short. I have been warned about her face, the spider bites, but still it's a shock. Her hair is a shock. I had reminded myself, but I had forgotten its hard yellow. She's very sunburned, she keeps her hair down around her face, her long yellow hair down around her face so we can't see her spider bites, her splotchy sunburned face, her blue eyes.

She won't come to us. She hides with another girl, her new friend Becca. They hang around together near the wall, giggling together by the wall. Ben and I go over to them and I think: Don't say anything about her face. She's still giggling, she's nervous, hunching over the way she does when she's nervous. I think it's okay, she's shy with us, and I remind myself again not to say anything about her face when all of a sudden she whips around at me like a snake strikes. "Don't touch me! Don't get near me! No!"

I back away.

"It takes a little time," Rebecca says to me in her cheerful way. What does she know? All around us all the other parents are hugging their children. And Ben and I can't even touch each other. We're so long divorced. We're so far apart after all these years. Ben stands there foolishly holding his canvas bag with the stuffed animals he brought for the occasion. He comes forward, holding it out to her, the way he used to give her presents when he came at Christmas. "This is for you," he says shyly, just the way he used to give them his shy presents, these children he so loves.

She takes the stuffed cat, holds it in the crook of her arm, and moves away from us.

Around us everyone is still hugging and exclaiming and exchanging news from home.

Ben and I look at each other. I can't move my face.

"All right, people, let's all take our places. We're going to talk about the experience a little bit, and then we have a slide show of the trip." Rebecca hustles us back to our places.

The counselor whom I've talked to on the phone comes over to us. "You're Augusta's parents?"

"Yes." We nod guiltily.

"She's going to make you pay," he says to us. "She's pretty angry."

"About what?" Ben asks like a dummy.

"You know, about the school. We just told her last night she's going to Forest Ridge. She's pretty mad."

We nod again. I'm scared Ben will back out.

Everyone sits down. Ben and I scooch closer with our chairs to where Augusta huddles in with Becca. They're still giggling.

Each of the children is supposed to say something about the Wilderness experience. Something they are proud of. Augusta's best of all. She is so clear as she describes a moment going up a steep place, describes precisely how she felt. And I think it was worth the $7,000—just for this. She's different inside. I can tell something's different. Don't think about her face, I tell myself. The big red splotches and the sunburned skin. It will heal I'm sure. Don't think about the

155

way she's acting. You're doing the right thing. And anyway, I ask myself: What's the alternative?

The slide show features the happy kids. The happy kids camping. The happy kids working, digging out a ditch. The happy kids rappelling. Hiking. Climbing. Wearing safety helmets. Climbing into tents. Climbing out of tents. Eating by a fire. Walking down a road. The kids getting into the van. The kids getting out of the van. There are a lot of slides. They're playing "What a Wonderful World" in the background and every time the song comes to an end it loops around and starts up again. The first time it is touching and pathetic and I feel my eyes fill up with tears. But by the third repetition of the song I stifle in myself the need to giggle. It's too much, the parking lot in Dalton, the long airplane rides, the heat, the city of Boise, the hotel rooms, the long distance phone calls, the splotched daughter, the old husband, the other parents with their understanding eyes, Rebecca's linen dress, the Danish pastries. The endless and relentless looping song, the happy kids in helmets going up the cliff, going down the cliff, getting into the van, getting out of the van, getting in.

The lights come on. It's finally over.

"Now I want you to break into groups—each student with his or her parents, sit close together with your knees touching—and I will come around and meet with each family," announces Rebecca. "And we'll talk about your experience and about what comes next.

"Augusta," she looks at my daughter, "can you do that?"

Augusta stares at her. I know that stare.

That's the dinner table stare. That's the one, all right.

They go off together into the hall, Augusta before her, ushered out. Rebecca comes in a little later. All the other parents are already gathered sitting knee to knee with their returned children. One of the counselors has taken away the little lonely fat boy, and Becca's gone off.

"I think she'll talk to you," Rebecca tells us. She's in charge now. That is clear.

"I told her she needs to stick to the rules."

The buzz of the room is enormous. All the parents talking to their kids. All the kids excited, answering.

"I told her if she gets inappropriate with you, then she's going to leave right away. That this is her chance to share with you about her experience. That if she can't do it in a healthy way she'll have to get in the van and we'll drive directly to the school."

Ben and I nod dumbly. We feel like we've been bad.

We sit down, closer than we've sat together in years. Augusta comes dragging in with her hair down around her face, sits with us, doesn't look at us, keeps her hair down.

Rebecca calls to all of us from the front of the room.

"All right. I want you parents to now tell your children why you sent them here to Wilderness."

It's our turn. I go first.

"Augusta, we were so worried. I didn't know what to do. I felt that I couldn't keep you safe. You wouldn't let me. I wanted you to be safe. I always love you and I miss you but I had to make you safe."

She glares at me from behind her yellow hair.

"Now Ben." Rebecca is beside us. "Now you tell Augusta why you sent her here."

"Well, Augusta. You know we love you and we want you to be safe. We thought this would be a good program for you. That you'd learn—" His voice cracks. He hates this so much. This kind of stuff. This is why we got married, not to do this. Why we got divorced. Our truest link. Feeling like oddballs while all around us everybody is mumbling obediently, all the parents, all the children, we the three disjointed ill-fitting ones from Maine, stumbling wrongly through our lines, not getting it right, not fitting in, splotchy and uncomfortable and strange.

"Now I want you students to tell your parents how you feel about the Wilderness experience that you just went through."

Augusta isn't talking.

Everybody else is talking. But not Augusta.

Rebecca looms near.

Augusta flips her hair back, shows us her blotched and ruined face, her sunburned peeling poisoned spider-bitten face—the red streaks standing out from the big patches. "Look at this!" she tells us. "Look at my face! They say it's never going to heal! It's my face! It's going to be like this forever 'cause the skin dies. And you did it to me. You sent me here. I was fine. You say you want me safe. You sent me here. I wasn't safe. And Forest Ridge isn't safe. I know about it. They lock you up. They take things that you say and turn them around, they get you to say things you don't mean, they make you dig ditches and carry stones, and they tell your parents it's a certain way but it's not that way. It's not for people like me. It's for rich people. Why don't you just let me go? Look! This is what I did the second day!"

And she pulls back her sleeve and then she shows us in one brief flash, before she yanks it down again, two red raised ridges on her arm where she's cut herself. Two long vertical streaks, two angry ridged red lines on her little wrist. On her pale soft skin.

I can't speak. I can't say anything. It feels like someone is choking me. I can't speak.

Ben says, "Oh Augusta!" but he can't speak either.

We can't look at each other.

We can't speak.

Rebecca comes over.

"So, how's this going?" she says in her cheerful way.

But we can't speak.

"Are you done?"

But we can't answer her.

I'm choking. I can't speak.

"All right. Well, I think we'll have some lunch now. There's a buffet set up in the hall. Augusta, why don't you go out and get something? And I want to talk to your parents for a while."

I manage this: "I love you, Augusta." But she won't look back.

Then Ben and I look at each other's faces.

Rebecca knows there's something.

"How'd it go?"

"Not good," I tell her dully. "Why didn't anybody tell us?"

"About her face? You knew about her face."

"About her wrist."

"What about her wrist?" she asks me sharply.

"She cut her wrist. She said the second day."

"I didn't know that." Rebecca presses her lips together, speaks to us sharply as if it's our fault. With our problem daughter.

"You know, this is pretty serious," she says.

No shit! I'm thinking wildly. No kidding!

"I'm not sure Forest Ridge is going to be able to work with Augusta. She may be too . . ."

She doesn't have the word. I fill it in. Extreme? Too much? Too crazy for Forest Ridge? Too *what?*

We talk a little. I don't know what I'm saying. I'm just crying now. "I couldn't talk when she was yelling at us. I couldn't answer. I couldn't say anything. It was like when she was home and she'd get going. I'm a person who can always talk. That's what I do. I talk way too much. But when she goes at me like that I can't talk."

Ben doesn't say anything. Sits there in silence.

I wish that we could hold each other's hands. But it's too late for that. We're both alone.

"Well, I'm going to look into this," Rebecca tells us. "But I do have to warn you that Augusta seems to be a very troubled young lady. And we'll take her over to Forest Ridge, that's the plan. But it may be that we'll have to recommend another place for her. Somewhere where she can get better treatment. For what her needs are."

"Will we see her again?" Ben asks.

"In September, at the parent seminar," she tells us.

"Now."

"Well, I think we need to get going to Forest Ridge, but she's probably in the hallway if you want to say good-bye to her."

We go out. Augusta lets Ben get near. He hands her another stuffed animal, a squirrel this time, and a paperback book.

I try to get closer but she holds her hands out. "No."

So I just leave, go back through the chilly air-conditioned room where we waited all morning. Where some of the parents are still talking with their children, hugging them. Some of the children are going home with their parents. Others are saying good-bye. I walk past them, past the little counselor with his elfin face.

"How'd it go?" he asks me, but I only shake my head.

16

"WHAT TIME'S your plane?" Ben asks me in the lobby.

I'm already checked out, but my plane doesn't leave until evening.

"At seven," I say. "I'm flying to Salt Lake City, spending the night there, leaving tomorrow morning at six A.M. for Boston."

"God," he says.

"I know."

"You want to walk downtown?" I ask him.

"Walk downtown?" he asks me like a dummy. "It's really hot out."

"I don't care. I need to walk."

"Okay," he says. "I'm going swimming anyway, downtown. There's a Y. I found it last time. When we came."

I go into the bathroom and change into shorts and a tank top, put my wallet in a hiker's fanny pack, and stick the rest of my stuff in my suitcase behind the desk.

He's changed too. Two middle-aged baboons in shorts and T-shirts going out into the Boise heat.

It's so hot when we go out of the hotel. It's like getting mugged.

"How far is it?" I ask him.

"A couple of miles. Are you sure you want to do this?"

"Yeah."

I'm really sure. I want to burn it out of me. Burn out the memory of my daughter's splotchy face. Burn out her anger. Burn out my sorrow. I hope the heat is like some sort of disinfectant that can burn out what I saw on my daughter's wrist.

We walk side by side down a sidewalk that isn't really meant for walking, past garages, little drive-in restaurants, car repair, liquor stores. She's heading in the van to Oregon.

"What do you think?" Ben asks me.

"I think she's really in bad shape," I tell him. "It kills me to see her like this."

"I know."

We're like survivors, Ben and I. I feel like we're walking out of a plane crash in this white heat. It's all unreal. Too much travel. Too many different hotel rooms. Too many airports and vans. Too many weird restaurants. Too much sun.

I tell him my latest theory, which is that Augusta is so full of dark swirling disorganized pain and fury that she uses everything—parties, sex, drugs, running, cigarettes, oblivion—to push it away. It sounds reasonable. But what do I know? I know it was true for me. Or I've decided that it was. But what do I really know about my own daughter?

"Do you think this place can help her?" he asks me.

He asks questions like that all the time. It makes me crazy. Like I know. I don't know. I don't want to have to convince him. I'm not convinced myself. I don't know. I'm paying for it. But I don't know.

"We're doing something," I tell him fiercely, stopping for

a moment on the hot street. I feel dizzy. "At least we're doing something."

"Yeah," he says.

We stop and drink huge glasses of lemonade and water at a drive-in. I think we must look weird. I imagine we look as if we're splattered with blood and wreckage. Smudge-smeared faces. Torn clothing. Dusty shoes. But probably we just look like two red-faced Eastern tourists with our shorts and T-shirts and my ridiculous fanny pack. We probably look like we're an old married couple instead of what we are—divorced parents of a suicidal daughter. I don't care. I don't care about anything. I'm just walking it out, walking to downtown Boise in the hot sun of a hot summer day, just moving forward.

In the center of the downtown, shaded by the buildings, he says, "I'm going over there. That's where I'm swimming. What are you going to do?"

I tell him I'll find a bookstore. I'll look around. Then I'll walk back.

"Be careful," he tells me, like it matters. "It's pretty hot."

No shit.

He goes off down the street on the shady sidewalk without looking back. He'll swim. That makes him feel better.

I walk down one street and up another. I can see how this is the kind of downtown you could fall in love with. Radio promotions. Downtown festivals. The wide lawns in front of the government buildings. A couple of nice sculptures. Empty streets. Nice shops. Revitalized. A nice museum. Closed today, of course. It's Saturday. It's afternoon and things are closing early. But I find a nice cool bookstore with a shady feel and long shelves of books. I look around at the Idaho authors, the Western lore and the Western authors, the new books and the old books, the poetry and the fiction.

I look around but I can't concentrate. There isn't any book I want to read.

The road back goes over a river. I stand on the bridge and look down at all the people riding down the river. They're all half naked. They're all smiling. Families. Young guys and pretty girls on huge inflated inner tubes, on rafts, in little boats, all riding down the brownish water of the river this hot day. Some of them have music playing and I hear it becoming more distinct as it gets closer; old summer songs coming in closer and then fading as they pass under the bridge and away off down the river into Idaho. Many of them are looking up into the sky as they pass by and they see me looking down and they smile. They wave up at me standing there on the hot bridge looking down. There are trees with big dusty leaves on either side of the river and I am grateful for the river, grateful for the people riding down.

A few blocks farther I think I'm going to faint. Everything's glittering and my head pounds with the heat. I feel as if I've got a fever.

I stop in McDonald's and go into the bathroom and look at my face in the mirror. It's bright red, as red as Augusta's ruined face. I splash on some water. Then I go out and I order french fries and a big glass of lemonade. The large size, I tell them, and when it comes I pay with hot money. Hot little coins the opposite of winter coins in Maine, so cold you think the cold will burn your fingers.

I sit down and I eat those french fries at the little McDonald's table. And I drink that big cup of lemonade. It tastes terrific. The salty salt, the cold, cold lemonade. And I think, if Augusta were here now she'd love the saltiness of the french fries. She'd love getting the giant-size lemonade. And Jack would make too much noise drinking his lemonade and she'd tell him to stop it and he'd look at me. And I would no longer think that little squabble was such a big deal. I wouldn't freak out and snarl at them or smack my hand on the table. I'd look up mildly from my own little tray and smile lovingly at their quarrel. Lovingly! I would be so delighted just to have them both in the same place with me, both healthy, both eating food that I had provided to them. Both my children. Both safe. Both where I could see.

The plane out of Boise to Salt Lake City flies into its lunar landscape just at sunset. The colors of the sunset are strange dark desert rose and dark orange. I think again of my children. How they'd like to see this place. How they'd point out the windows of the plane. Why didn't I take them to more places when they would still go with me? Why didn't I take more trips? More time off? Have more money? Now I am spending money I don't even have. Money for expensive programs. Money for the Wilderness. Money to fly out and see the school. Money for hotels and rented cars. I should have spent that money on other things. Fun things. Things we could have done together if I hadn't always been working, if I hadn't always been worried. If I hadn't always been broke.

I land in Salt Lake City, get to my hotel room when it's dark and already late. I don't even want anything to eat, I just want to get to my room. No fajitas tonight. No wine. No french fries. Just my room. I don't even bother to claim it with unpacking. I'll be up at four and out again by five. I sleep barely five hours, once I've toured the useless channels of the television set in this latest hotel room while my daughter arrives somewhere in Oregon in the van and is tumbled out and is put in one—which one of the cabins? Which one of the girls is looking at her? Is wondering about her scalded face? Is making a remark about my daughter with her red splotchy face? Her yellow hair? Her angry angry eyes?

◈

My flight's delayed the next morning. I could have slept another hour. I never check. Now I just sit in a chair in the row of hard plastic chairs, stunned with too much emotion, too many rooms, too many days on the road, in the air, ready to be home.

Across from me there's a little family. A small Asian woman and her husband are traveling with a little daughter, maybe one and a half. She's all dressed up in her little summer outfit with her shiny black hair cut in bangs all around her head and her cute little round face. She runs to her mother and then runs off and then turns around with a flirty look and I watch her and she is so darling and I think about my own girl and that's it.

I have to talk to someone.

I go to the pay phone and I call my sister in New York, but my brother-in-law answers the phone and tells me she's not there and suddenly, poor guy, I'm telling him about the little Japanese girl and about my own girl and her wrist! I tell him how she cut herself. I tell him how her wrist was all cut up with big ridges and how she said she did it the second day there.

And he says I know, I know, even though he doesn't know, and he asks if I'm all right. I give one of those crazy-sounding giggles through my tears because of course I'm not all right. My little girl tried to kill herself. She cut her own wrist. And I wasn't there. And all I wanted was to make her safe.

Once I'm crying I can't stop, leaning my hot forehead

against the little cold metal patch on the pay phone, phone pressed against my ear, hearing my brother-in-law's voice in New York speaking to me quietly, sadly from so far away. I know, he keeps saying, I know. It's very hard. And Oh, like a breath exhaled. He's a doctor, after all, he's seen it all. Families in such pain.

Then I push away my tears, the way you do, and say goodbye and tell him yes, I'll call when I get home. I wash my face in the ladies' room trying not to look at myself in the wide mirror, trying not to meet anyone else's eyes. I have to get back, get my bag, get on the plane, get home.

Maine. Summertime. I plunge into it like a lake on a hot day. I go to work. I am very busy. Jack's got his job, and he's busy, too. Every day he goes out, handsome in his handsome ferry uniform: his clean khakis, his billed cap.

And I go to work. I've got a lot to do. I'm on the phone. I'm selling spots. The ratings are up. I'm working hard. I'm going to bring Don Imus back to the Bangor Civic Center in October for a special broadcast: *Live from Bangor, Maine!* Bob and Sheri to the new Filene's opening at the Bangor Mall. We're way up over last year. I'm a success.

At night I take calls from Oregon, reassuring calls from the school. She's there. She's all right. She's settling in. She's doing what she needs to do. She's not glad to be there, no, but she's there, I tell myself. She's there, I tell myself. She's safe.

They tell me she's participating. They tell me they have taken her to a doctor for her face. They don't want to ask her about the wrist yet. She needs to establish trust. But she's fine, they tell me.

167

We have our first conference call on a speakerphone with her counselor-mentor, Rose. The counselor asks Augusta a question. Augusta is supposed to tell us why she is there. She is angry. She starts yelling. She is crying; she is yelling at us. And I can't think of anything to say.

They tell us she's doing fine, that this is to be expected, but they don't say why. I think maybe she's crazy.

Sometimes my boyfriend comes down, but he's always angry at me now. He says he feels bereft of me, and I don't care. I wish he'd just let go of me. I'm tired of his exhausting desire to be kind while he is so angry at me, angry for my screwed-up life, angry at me for my troubles, angry at me for being so busy with my own things, angry at me because I don't care enough about him, think enough about him, want to be with him enough, desire him, love him enough. We fight ceaselessly uselessly and it feels like just a matter of time until we quietly unravel all the years. I can't even remember why I ever liked him in the first place. We have nothing in common. He bores me. I enrage him. We are done.

I don't want to work things out, talk things out. I just want to go to work, to come home, to walk in the evenings when it isn't raining, to walk early in the morning, to read my book, to write letters to my daughter, to wait for everything to get better, to wait and to move forward dully through my life. I am too full of my own troubles and worries and confused emotions to bother with his. I am angry at her, I am protective of her. I am worried about her, I am furious with her. I am scared, sad, hurt, and I am secretly delighted that she's not just some dumb sheep. Through it all I love her. I love her. She is my daughter. She is not his daughter. So he has only the aggravation and the worry and impatience and her anger toward him and I don't care what he's feeling because I'm feeling too much by myself.

But it's also quieter, with her away.

My life is like a little pond with a boat in it.

My life is like a little clean path on a straight line through the woods.

I put things down and there they are again, next morning, still right there.

There are no longer any big emergencies in the middle of the night. I know where everybody is.

My father comes to supper one summer evening. He's down this way and has a free evening so he asks me out to supper, but I say why don't you come over here and I'll fix something? I plan something out of *Betty Crocker's Good & Easy Cookbook* that involves skinless boneless chicken breasts and lime juice and salsa and zucchini. It's quite good and seems, in fact, much better than it is.

We have cold white wine that is so plain it tastes almost like very cold water.

I get lemon ice for dessert.

He's proud of me, my father. The executive. The cook. The tall girl.

He compliments me on the food and on my house and on my good sense with the children.

Then he asks about Augusta. We both know not to tell my mother everything. Even now, even when things seem relatively safe, she tells me she still can't sleep. She tells me she cries when she writes to Augusta. So I haven't told her all of it. I haven't told her about my daughter's wrist.

It's the cold center, the sight of my daughter's wrist. It's at the very middle of the pain. The nugget of dry ice inside the swirl of smoke and vapor. It's what you dare not touch.

I keep coming close to it in my mind and skittering away.

I've told almost no one. It's my own.

But tonight after supper, buoyed by the dry wine and the good food and the quiet summertime kitchen (everything in its place, all the dishes in their racks, the clean floor, the tidy cabinets with their flowered handles), I approach it.

"I have to tell you something," I say.

My father looks at me with his alert reporter's look like a bird, head a little tilted so he'll hear every word. Ready to take notes.

And then I tell him. I tell him about the real visit, not the edited version I have given them—the trip to Idaho, the heat in Boise. I tell him about how my daughter's face looked splotchy and ruined. I tell him about my daughter's wrist when she pushed back her sleeve. I go get the little flowered notebook I found when I was cleaning out her room and read him the passage about cutting her face when she was only in the eighth grade. Two years ago! Almost three years ago! When she was just a kid. How deep it goes.

He listens carefully and he doesn't say much.

"Don't tell Mother," I tell him. "I didn't want to tell Mother."

"I wish you hadn't told me," he says.

I feel relieved at telling him. But then I worry about how much I've put on him. How much she's put on all of us. More than we can stand. We're rickety. She doesn't know this yet. We're rickety little tables heaped already with our own heaps. How can we keep taking more?

That ends the evening, though we wash up together and

even take a little walk together around the quiet summer-time block.

"You're doing the right thing," my dad tells me. "You're doing just right."

The counselor calls from the school. Rose. She tells me Augusta is settling in. She's starting to talk about what she was into at home. Lots of pot. Acid. Drinking. Dealing drugs. "Oh yeah," Rose tells me, "she's got her story."

We have another phone conference and Augusta cries and tells me she doesn't want to be there. That I don't understand. That it's awful there. That nobody's like her. They're all rich. They're all preppies. She doesn't want to stay there. "Let me come home!" she says. "Let me come home!"

I tell myself that she's alive. That she's not high. That she's not in jail. That she is safe.

It seems like such small comfort.

But what else? What else can I do?

Some old friends come up from New York City and we take a walk together and I know I'm an awful friend right now. I don't even try to be nice. I won't talk about certain things. They ask about Augusta and I say I can't talk about it. And they ask about Jack and I say no no I can't talk about him either. And when they try to tell me about their own kids I change the subject. I don't want to hear about their daughter or how their son is doing at Yale. They tell me they are planning a family trip to Jamaica in the winter holidays; I don't want to hear any of it. And I don't want to tell them anything

171

because this little cup I carry full to the brim is so fragile. I don't want to slosh it. I don't want to spill it. I don't want to drop it, smash it. So we have kind of an odd hike and then a rather unpleasant dinner, waiting too long for the mediocre food, running out of approved subjects because I don't really want to talk about anything at all.

I have a huge horrible fight with my boyfriend. I am so wired and strung so tight. Everything he says drives me crazy. Everything he does makes me insane. One night Jack is going to stay at his grandparents' and we are invited to a party. They are his friends. Fine. I'll go. I get dressed up in my summer skirt. White rumply linen. My yellow shirt. Great. I look great. But at the party he's mad at me. Something I said. I don't care. I know exactly what it was. When I asked him for another drink and he told me in a serious, kind, fatherly voice, "You won't be happy if you have another drink," and I told him that was the dumbest thing I'd ever heard. Because *(a)* doesn't he get it? I'm never going to be happy as long as my daughter is in Oregon in treatment, as long as my daughter yells at me on the phone, as long as my daughter hates me, and *(b)* how does he know what makes me happy? and *(c)* just get me the fucking drink. So I say in a mean way, "Don't tell me what to do," and he lets out a big furious breath like a dark wind and gets up and walks away and then won't come back again and I sit there in my summer clothes and talk to other people and laugh at what we say—ha ha ha—and I don't even care, let him go walk around pretending to talk to other people! Let him go off and ignore me when I'm at his stupid friends' stupid party! I kind of hate him anyway so who cares? My daughter hates him. She used to beg me not to marry him, and I was always careful not to promise, though in my heart I knew I could never marry anyone again. Now I really know that I would never marry him, this grouchy bastard with his stupid glasses and his stupid pants that are too short, walking around talking to this one and that one and not even glancing back.

We used to be great. I used to be amazed at my good fortune—this handsome, big, smart man who loved me. But now he just gets on my nerves and is like another chore that doesn't interest me. And now I am never enough for him. I'm never available enough, I'm never able to go where he wants to take his girlfriend—Europe, sailing, parties, Boston. I'm either working or else I'm in some disaster with my children. He's sick of it and I'm sick of him and I'm sick of his inability to help. When I call him from out of the midst of the jungle of my horrible life, crying in some frantic fight with my daughter, who is screaming at me from her room or cutting her wrists in Idaho, or my son, who is getting kicked out of school by the woman with the googly eyes, he says the same thing, always the same thing.

"Oh honey," he tells me. "Oh I wish there was something I could do."

Then, just to make me madder: "I really do."

He always listens on the other end of the phone far away in his house and he says yeah, I know. I want to kill him. I want to yell into his ears. He can't help me. Nobody can help me.

"When am I ever going to see you?" he asks me just to enrage me further.

All right—you're seeing me tonight—here we are! We're sitting close together with his arm around me watching the fireworks on the water in the summer night. It should be ro-

mantic, only it's not. We don't like anything. We are both too
sad, because here we are and we are enemies at last.

Next morning, in his sunny house, I try to make peace with
him. I say, "Let's go sailing."

I hate to sail, and he knows it, but he loves it. He keeps
thinking that I'll change my mind. After nine years, you'd
think he would catch on, but there it is.

But this morning, after the fireworks and the parties and
the little argument that simmers away undiscussed on the
back burner, I suggest we go sailing.

So we head on the boat and it's a splendid day and right
away we are back in the fight.

I start it after he makes some little tiny remark.

"Don't tell me what I like," I say, out there on the perfect
water.

"God. You sound like my old wife," he replies.

"Don't tell me I sound like your wife," I tell him.

And we're off. It's a horrible fight. We're not yelling, but
we're really mad. We say we're mad about all the mean little
remarks, the little pointed comments, little jabs, but we're
really mad about other stuff. I'm mad because my life's in a
shambles and he just gets to go sailing. He's mad because he
just wants to be with me to have things nice to go places but
I'm always too busy or too crazy or have some crisis in my
life. We fight and we fight and we fight and then I start crying. Down below, I lie down on the hard little benchy bed inside the belly of the boat and I cry harder than I have since
Augusta left. I start out crying for our ruined affair and for
his meanness and my fury and having to be stuck for what
feels like the rest of my life on this stupid boat, but I wind up

crying for everything—for my daughter's wrist, for her blotchy face, for her fury with me, for my lost ruined life, for all my friendships stolen out from under me while I was busy trying to keep my own life from capsizing. I cry and I cry and there is no bottom to all my tears, no horizon, just this enormous endless sorrow so that whenever I start to grind to a choky halt a fresh wave of crying hits me and I cry and I cry some more.

Before this I was broken, but I was still moving forward. I was still giving my mother reports from the front that sounded plausible, that didn't sound too bad. Serious, but not too bad. I was still going to work every day. I was still making the phone calls, getting to the appointments, sending the packages. I was still on top, as they say, of things. But now I feel split, the brokenness spilling out in untidy heaps, my face streaked with tears pressed against the rubbery vinyl of the bench cushion, hot and wet and sticky, and I can't stop. I feel as if I will never stop crying.

Later we shakily depart the boat and drive soberly back to his house. We have decided to "try" for another month. We say we'll give it until Labor Day, but we both know we're done. He can't take it. My despair. My horrible life. And I can't have anyone in it who doesn't love Augusta as much as I do. It just doesn't work. My ex-husband makes more sense than my boyfriend right now. At least he's part of it. They're his children. It grinds at him the way it grinds at me. He understands how impossible it is to carry on, to have a life, to talk/think about anything else when your daughter has red welts, red streaks all over her face, when there are those red ridges on your daughter's wrist, when your daughter is far away and can only scream from Oregon that she hates you, hates you, hates you.

We drive back and we don't talk much. I'm a hollow thing.

I sit in the truck, high up, glittery day all around. This could be the beginning. This air. This truck. This man beside me. It could be eight years ago and I could be so in love and so dizzy with the perfect day and the clean snap of the sail and the tired feeling coming home dazed with sun, but instead I'm just hollow and broken and dim.

"So, I'll see you later," he tells me as I get into my own car.

"Yeah."

But we both know it's going to be a while.

17

THAT NIGHT ROSE calls from Forest Ridge. "I have to tell you something," she tells me. She tells me Augusta has said she was raped.

Her little legs.

"I haven't got the whole story yet," Rose says. "She doesn't want to talk about it. She just mentioned something, real fast. I caught it."

She doesn't know anything else. She says she'll let me know when she learns more. She says they don't want to push Augusta. That she needs time.

I know right away who it was. That terrible boy with the dead eyes on Main Street last summer. The shadowy voice on the phone.

I call my boyfriend.

I call Ben.

I don't know what else to do. I want to kill the boy. But I can't go kill the boy.

I call my sister.

I want her to react the way she did two years ago when Augusta first told me she wasn't coming home. When *that* seemed like such a blow. God. I called my sister and she yelled! She yelled for my pain! She said, "Oh my God, oh Martha. Oh my God."

I want someone to feel crazy the way I feel crazy, hearing this.

But this time there have been so many big things. So many crises. And she has, after all, her own problems. So when I call she says only "Oh, really?" as if I'm telling her I bought a new sweater.

"Really? Do you think it's true?" she asks.

I don't answer.

"Why doesn't that surprise me?" she muses. "Hmm!"

I have to go.

I am furious with my sister.

I am furious.

I can't do anything. That's what I feel most of all. I've always been able to do something. To talk. Or to yell, or to walk off somewhere; walk really hard. I've always been able to fix things or to figure things out. But I can't do anything for my daughter. What can I do for my daughter? There is more and there is more and there is more and there is always more and it is too much. It is too much.

My therapist is a kind, quiet man and the room where we meet is peaceful. The walls are painted gray. There are the photographs of his family. There are the books and the quiet pictures and the lamp and the little gray couch where I sit, and the chair where he sits, and the door. He likes to make jokes. He makes a joke about my sailing day. He thinks I'm being spoiled—sailing, not liking sailing, being so hard on my boyfriend, getting so mad.

But then, like someone peeling back their sleeve to show their wound, I tell him the rest of it. I try to show him the extent of my despair. I'm desperate, and as I talk about what has been going on, I keep circling toward the word that Rose said to me on the phone just the other night but I can't say it. And I can't say how my sister sounded, preoccupied, unsurprised, busy.

I can't say it.

I can only say how I feel. Isn't that how it's supposed to work? Isn't that the idea, you say how you feel and someone listens to you and somehow that makes it better?

He says, "Okay. Okay." And he tells me to just keep walking. And he tells me I'm doing what I can do. He tells me to come back in two weeks and he puts his arms around me, holds me for a moment against his blue sweater, and I leave.

I think about that embrace, driving home from work late that afternoon. Is he supposed to be hugging me? It's a beautiful long evening. I wonder what it meant. I keep driving, taking the long way home, down the Bayside Road. The light is wonderful. It's Maine. It's the middle of August. It hasn't rained since June. I drive with my sunroof open and the air comes through the car and the radio is on, playing the oldies, songs I know by heart. I realize I am thinking about something different. I am thinking about the music. I am thinking about the summer. I am not thinking about my daughter. I am worrying. But I am not worrying about my daughter. I am worrying about my therapist's embrace.

That afternoon, before even going home, I climb Acadia Mountain. But this time it's different.

I go very fast up the trail I know almost by heart. The rocks have stories written on them. The time I went with an old boyfriend one winter twenty years ago and we slid on the ice and it reminded him of Thumper in the movie *Bambi* and we both thought that was hilarious. The time I went in early fall with Augusta. It seemed like a big mountain, maybe too big for her, but she said she wanted to go and she kept up, went fast, went ahead of me wearing her bright blue satin jacket. I told her a story the whole way up and the whole way down with plenty of cannibalism because that's what she liked. And on the way back, on the woods road, we scuffed and scuffed in the dry October leaves. The time five years later when I ran up the side of this same mountain because I didn't think I could stand to be in my house one more minute after some fight with my daughter I don't even remember now. Tonight I am somewhere between all of the stories, outside all of the stories.

My boyfriend and I go to Nova Scotia and spend two days driving through what feels like Maine thirty years ago; the little towns, the quiet country roads, the sea beside. We say we would like to live here. We imagine our lives in Nova Scotia. Driving to Halifax for a movie. Picnicking in Peggy's Cove.

We reach a sort of sad truce one night in our hotel room. Things will never be right again, but we'll stay together. That's what it feels like. Things will never be right.

I dream that I am with my children and they are young and we are in a big house at the foot of a mountain. And they are young again and love me and I am pushing them around the house in a shopping cart and they are so darling. And Augusta is so sweet and young and she hugs me and wants to sit by me and read stories. Her eyes are beautiful! She leans against me and she is loving and sweet. Jack comes over and the three of us are together. I am so happy in my dream.

When I get back to work, I call my broker. I've decided to sell the business. For the last two years, off and on, I've been getting offers, but I've never really wanted to sell until now. The landscape of radio is changing. Little companies are being bought up by big, publicly traded companies. Prices are high. They might not get higher. At first, when I thought about it I hated the thought. I liked my job. I liked my life: living in Maine, raising my children, running the family radio stations. But now everything's changed. Nothing's the way it was. I don't want to go digital. I don't want to buy more stations. I don't want to take on more debt. I don't want to take tickets at the New Year's Eve Oldies Dance Party at the Holiday Inn in the year 2000, 2001. I don't know what I want to do. But I don't want to do this anymore. This is what I did in the other part of my life. I'm afraid I'll get stranded here in Ellsworth with my radio stations when all other radio stations are owned by big companies. That's the sensible reason, but the real reason is this: I don't want to sit behind this desk anymore. I want a different life.

"I'll see what I can do," he tells me. Good.

Rose calls again. This time she says Augusta says she wasn't raped, that Rose misunderstood her. Whoops. She says she and Augusta are getting close. That Augusta will come and sit on her lap.

"She isn't ready to talk to you yet," she tells me.

"But she'll be ready by the time you come out," she says.

There's a parent seminar in September. I'm going out. Ben's going out. Jack will stay with my parents.

I have my reservations and my tickets already.

It's a month away.

I don't really know what's going on in Oregon. I have to trust these people. To trust that they know what they're doing. The information that I get keeps changing, but the basic rules stay the same. The kids have to wear certain clothes. They have to go to group. They go through what they call "Life Steps." I'm not sure what they do in the Life Steps, but they say that the Life Steps transform the children. She's having her first Life Step now. She's going to "come clean" to us when we come in September. She's going to tell us all the stuff she did before she went there.

When we go out there we will have two days of parent seminars when they explain the school to us, when we meet the staff. Then we will get to see Augusta. She will be able to come out with us. She will have signed agreements—what she gets to do, what she can't do. I'm scared.

Jack and I have developed our own little routine since Augusta's been gone, but school will be starting soon and we both dread it.

"I hate school," Jack tells me.

"I know," I say. "I'm working on it."

We eat little suppers and he puts away the dishes after I've washed them.

He drives me around the town after it gets dark. He's not supposed to, but he is very cautious, and I like this time we have together, me sitting in the passenger seat, him tall and proud in the driver's seat with the seat pushed way back to accommodate his long legs, and the car moving slowly through the quiet evening. We go down our road, around down by the harbor, back up to our house. He always thanks me.

"Thank you," he says, "for letting me drive."

He's still a little angry about his sister. He doesn't think she ought to be there. He doesn't like what I tell him about the rules. That she can't wear black clothes. That she can't listen to certain music, can't talk to her friends, can't wear her chains around her neck. "I don't see why," he says. But he does. He knows.

One day I'm in Bar Harbor sitting on a bench after a big hike watching people go by and Rain comes floating down the sidewalk in a long skirt. She swoops down upon me and kisses me.

"Martha!" she says.

She asks about Augusta.

I tell her Augusta is away for a while.

"Where is she?" she asks me. She's not so friendly now. "Can I write to her?"

"No. Not yet," I tell her. Not ever, is what I'm thinking.

"Why not?"

"She needs to work on some stuff."

I hate the language I'm using. But it's the language I'm stuck with. It's the dumb, awkward language of people in emotional crisis. What a phrase that is. I think Rain might understand all this going through my head, but I can't talk to her. She's mad at me now for taking my daughter away. For hiding my daughter away from her. For ruining their summer of being beautiful sixteen on the town. I ask her what she's up to. She's mad at me, but she tells me grudgingly that she's moved out. She's in an apartment. She's working in a bar.

"Are you allowed to do that?" I ask her.

"Oh well, nobody asks how old I am." She shrugs. "I look older."

She doesn't look older. She looks like my daughter's friend.

I feel tired and old sitting here with my gray woolly hair and my shorts and my old legs. Hiked out. Exhausted. The bad mother.

"So tell her I said hi!" Rain tells me. "Tell her I want to see her. I'm going west, you know. I'm going out to California in a few weeks."

"How are you getting there?" I ask her.

"Oh a bunch of us are buying a van."

I want to puke. I've traveled by van myself, of course, but now I'm the mother.

She smiles at me but it's a mean smile. She doesn't like me anymore. But she doesn't want to be angry. She wants to be all floaty and forgiving and wise. So she says good-bye in a kind high voice and floats away down the sidewalk in her long skirt, and I'm stuck there on the bench.

On the way home I stop by Jenny's. She's out in the yard, working. I haven't seen her in a few months. We've talked once or twice on the phone. She's Rain's mother.

She comes around the side of the house. Her hands are dirty from working in the garden. She's got a sunburn and an old shirt on. She's so pretty. She gives me a big hug.

"How you doing?"

"I just saw Rain."

"Oh, yes."

"She looks okay."

Jenny sighs. "She's okay. She's on her own. We just couldn't take it anymore. It got too crazy. So she's got a place with some people in Bar Harbor. I don't know. She says she wants to go to California in a van or something. I guess she has to find her way now. I have to let her. How's Augusta?"

I tell her about the school, about Wilderness, about everything. How it's been. I don't tell her everything. I don't tell her all the hard parts but she knows. She's got her own crazy daughter to remind her. She knows.

We look at each other ruefully.

"We ought to stay in touch," she tells me.

I know we should. She's right.

"We ought to check back in a couple of years and see how it worked out—both our ways," she tells me.

She's right. It doesn't matter what we do—the school, the Wilderness Program, the escorts, the regular school, the apartment in Bar Harbor, the van, California. It doesn't matter. We can't really fix anything. We can only do whatever we do and then wait and see. There's no way to fix things for certain, to make things go a certain direction.

She's right.

Driving home I'm reminded of something I said to Rose. I said, "I probably let it go too far."

I said, "But I thought I could fix it myself."

Hadn't I always been able to do everything? Paint the ceiling, climb the mountains, find the money, do all the jobs. Raise the children. Run the business. But I couldn't do this. That realization, as much as my pain for Augusta, is my pain in all of this. My own feeling of failure and defeat. I've failed with my daughter, and now I feel as if I can only fail at everything.

During the summer one of our old friends dies. He has been sick for a long time. Cancer. He was the younger brother of a friend of mine growing up. He was a wild boy and I hadn't seen him in years except in photographs so I think of him still eight years old with his bright eyes and his flop of long hair and his wild laugh.

I can hardly write to his mother. It's too familiar, what I need to say. It feels like what somebody could write to me. It makes me think what I would do if Augusta died.

All that summer, all that fall, in between work and selling the business and suppers with Jack and getting up in the morning and working at my desk and talking on the phone and visiting with my friends, in between appointments and grocery shopping and seeing my therapist and going to the dentist and getting my hair cut and going out to dinner, I am climbing mountains. The most real thing is walking. I go into the woods and I go up the mountains, and I go down the mountains, and sometimes I cry, and sometimes I make a kind of a moaning and grinding sound and sometimes I say things out loud, say: "All I wanted was for her to be safe," "I tried I tried I tried," "I did everything wrong," and sometimes: "Please let her be all right." But none of it really helps; none of it gets to the core of it. None of it gets to the inside of it, scratches the unbearable itch deep inside.

I go into her room when I get home. It's still Augusta's room, though I've cleaned it up. I left the pictures on the walls—the photographs of kittens, the cute boys from teen magazines, cute TV actors, models, singers. I left the psyche-delic sixties pictures reclaimed from my own old boxes in the attic. The bumper sticker in black on white, once very hip, a little tattered now, that says: *Join the Army. Travel to foreign lands. Meet exciting and interesting people. And kill them.* I have left it all up. The books on the shelves. The wreath of dried flowers. The photographs: Augusta in jazz band sitting on the floor with her sax, Augusta at Halloween with her face painted, her arm around her friend Alexis, Augusta at graduation with her eighth-grade class. The room seems full of her, and yet she's gone. Augusta, gone.

The summer seems to go on forever. I am never happy. Or I think I am starting to be happy but then something hap-pens and I lose it. Like the day when I am headed some-where—it's a bright day—headed probably out for a hike. I drive down the hill and the sun is shining through the sun-roof and the sky is blue and it is the end of the summer, the sweetest part of the summer, right around Labor Day when the last of the summer is so sweet, and I see Brenda and her son drive up a side road in their car. And I think: The twins are learning to drive already! I see Brenda sitting stiffly in the passenger seat and her son sitting up proud and tall be-hind the wheel of the car and they wave uncertainly to me. He must have his permit. All I want at that moment is to have my daughter here beside me, and to have her learning to drive with her proud permit, to be teaching my daughter to drive on this golden end-of-summer day. I put the back of my hand up to my mouth and God I'm crying again. I didn't know I had them in me, all those tears.

18

FINALLY IT'S TIME to go to Oregon for the parent seminar.

When I get out there I go to the hotel where all the parents stay. The Riverhouse. It's fine. My room has a nice bed. I unpack, putting everything away carefully, and I walk around the room. Yes. This will be fine.

In the morning they get us all into a big room. We have name tags with our names and the names of our children with colored stars to signify what school they're in. Lower school. Middle school. Upper school.

The room is decorated with photographs of the students. In all the photographs everyone is smiling. I can't find Augusta. She hasn't been there very long. At last I find one picture of her pulling on a rope at the tug-of-war. She is smiling her big smile. I look close but I can't tell if her face is still blotchy. She looks okay.

The parents all look like regular people. We mill around. Augusta has complained that everyone there is really rich but they don't look so rich to me. They look like regular people, some people I might be friends with, some people I would never get to know. They are mostly in twos. I find Ben and we sit together in the metal folding chairs when it is time to sit down. There are boxes of Kleenex everywhere. This is the drill. This is how these programs operate. Boxes of Kleenex. Parents in chairs.

We each have to stand up and say who we are and where we're from who's our kid and why we sent them here. Some people go on and on about it. The sassy older parents of the upper school have the red stars. They thank the school and say how grateful they are. They talk about the ups and downs from their long perspective. They say the school saved their children's lives, that they have no doubt. Some of them are taking their kids home for a visit. Some of them are getting ready to graduate the program. They are neater than the rest of us and they cry less. Some people just stand up and cry. I'm a crier. I started crying the minute I came into the room. So I say some lame thing about wanting my daughter to be safe and well and I try to explain about seeing the twins driving with their mother only it doesn't come out right. But later someone puts her arm around me and she's crying, too, and she says, I know just what you meant.

The staff sits at the back. They're an odd lot. I can't tell yet who is who but I spot Rose, who has been described to me as an "earth mother" and is, as I suspected, really fat.

Next comes the Head of the School. We're back in our folding chairs. She talks about how the school works. She brings us up-to-date. What the school's been doing. Who they've hired. Who's left. What new programs they're trying. She explains their philosophy, which involves drawing a circle on a big pad of paper on an easel with a Magic Marker. She apologizes for the lopsided shape of the circle. The circle represents our children's true spirit. Our children's pure soul. What the school believes in. It is implied that not everyone believes in the child's spirit.

Next she draws daggers and arrows coming from all sides, sticking at the pure round lopsided soul of our children. This is society. Society is different now, full of bad things. Bad movies. Bad music. Bad TV. Bad messages.

She draws another circle around the first circle. This is the shell our children build up to deal with the attacks of the daggers and arrows.

I'm with her. I'm taking notes. On my little pad I carefully draw my own lopsided circle, my own daggers and arrows, my own hard shell. Okay, I'm thinking all along, okay okay I get it. It's pretty simple. I like that it's simple. I like the Head's pale yellow dress sprinkled with small flowers. I like her handsome bearded husband with the accent who also works at the school, works with the older kids. The upper school.

Then she shows how, with a triangle shape, the school drives a wedge into the shell, gets at the pure calm center of our children. Gets through the shell, returns them to themselves. Lets them be themselves. Their best selves. That's what they do.

They don't believe in counseling, she tells us. Counseling hasn't worked for our kids. Psychiatrists and psychologists haven't worked for our kids. Experience works. So they try to take away the harmful influences. The bad music lyrics (can't listen to the radio), the awful movies (watch only nice movies there), the awful books. All the influences. And they do the Life Steps, which are experiential, and they do the groups, and they drive the wedge into our children's pure hearts to retrieve them.

Sounds good to me. I'm for it.

I glance around. The parents are all listening. They're for it too.

We are going to do our own mini version of a Life Step. We each choose someone in the room to be our buddy and I choose the little one from California. She's divorced too. She's also, I see by her blue star, in lower school.

We clump up close with our buddies. Ben got a sad woman with long hair. I hope no one has to dance with the teacher.

We are supposed to tell our buddies a big secret about ourselves. I tell my buddy I'm selling the radio stations. She tells me her child is her brother's son. I wish I had chosen a different buddy.

We go off. We are supposed to go off with our buddies and tell each other our lives. We are supposed to have lunch with our buddies. I'm thinking this isn't so bad. We get to talk about ourselves. This is what Augusta is doing all this time. I have heard parents say that they wish they were as self-aware as the students who go through the program. That the Life Steps teach them things they never learned until they were thirty, thirty-five. I think maybe I'll learn something. That it's kind of cool, this community of damaged parents.

My buddy and I go out to have lunch together. We find a little hip restaurant. Bend is full of little hip restaurants. They all serve big bread. They all serve odd cheeses. Fancy olives. Fine with me.

I go first. I tell the whole story—my childhood, my mother, my sister, my father, my craziness. Madeira. Drugs. Antioch. Travel. Brazil. I tell about moving to Maine and

191

writing. I tell about my mother's red lipstick and my wild big hair. I tell about boyfriends and marriage and having babies and getting divorced and going to work at the radio stations and getting good at it and learning about business. I tell about my suits and Rotary and being on boards. I tell her about selling it and changing it all—changing my life around again. I tell about losing my daughter.

I'm going on too long, so I wind down and Alex starts up. She matches me story for story, only her stories are much more extreme. Her crazy mother. Her crazy sex. Prison father. Drugs. I'm not sure I want to know all these things. She seemed so normal. I'm not sure I want her to be telling me all these different things. How come I have to get the crazy buddy? My own life with all its vividness, with all its tapestry, seems plain compared to hers.

The whole time we are eating our enormous sandwiches. Drinking our big drinks. Talking fast like you tell things to a brand-new friend, talking fast and interrupting, looking at our watches, gobbling our healthy sandwiches, bean sprouts coming out of our lips like we're eating bundles of hair, telling our stories in Bend, Oregon.

She keeps talking. It gets weirder. Picking up guys in a bar, sharing a hotel room with her mother, who is also picking up guys. Two brothers at a bar in New Orleans.

"That's pretty weird," I tell her.

"I know," she says to me. "I know. I think of it now and I think: what was I thinking?"

What *was* she thinking? I know what I'm thinking. I'm thinking she's nuts.

We get back in the car and drive back to the Riverhouse. It's time to go back in. The buddies are lined up. All the middle-aged parents standing at the entrance in the soft September afternoon. They are in obedient pairs like Noah's animals, like prisoners lined up in pairs. Some of them are holding hands. I don't want to go that far, but they have told us to take our buddy's hand and so I take her little hand in mine her soft little hand and, feeling foolish, stand with the other pairs of parents in the prison line. I wonder how we must look to the other patrons of the Riverhouse, the other people of Bend driving by and seeing this parade of parents holding hands, filing back into the big room.

They've prepared a Life Step jamboree for us. The staff must have been very busy while we were out there eating lunches. The room is dim. We're doing the Forever Young Life Step, which is meant to help us explore our childhoods. There are balloons in bunches hanging all around and streamers glittering and chairs set here and there in sets of two. There are toys and stuffed animals and posters on the walls and it is dim with colored lighting and soothing music. The guy who is the top head of the school comes in and he stands up there with a cordless mike and he tells us to all sit down because some naughty parents are still wandering around grabbing up the stuffed animals, stocking up on Kleenex, exclaiming over the children's books, the battered copies of *The Velveteen Rabbit* and *Winnie-the-Pooh*.

We all take our chairs and stare into our buddies' eyes as we've been told to do. The soothing music, relentlessly soothing, plays on and we are told to tell our buddies the things our mothers told us. The man with the mike keeps interrupting us, his amplified voice roaring out, "Momma told me! Momma told me!" I understand that I'm supposed to be really moved by this experience and share secrets from my childhood and get out all the rage from my childhood, from my own twisty adolescence, and I welcome the chance to get at whatever darkness in me swirls but it's too noisy and the music is too annoying and my buddy is too weird and anyway, as I tell her, looking into her dark little spaniel eyes, "I'm sure my mother made mistakes. I'm sure she told me things that weren't right, but I'm over all that now. It was too long ago. I love her. We're friends. Why dig it all up?"

And then we're supposed to tell other things—our dreams from our childhood, our favorite toy. Our memories. Our fathers.

I get what's going on. I understand that I am meant to be moved by this, and I *want* to be moved by this, I want to explore those deep regions and come to some new revelation, but let's face it—what else have I been doing for the last thirty years? All those journals. All those acid trips. All that time spent in the woods. All that time spent living alone writing thinking smoking writing thinking. All those rocky, solitary walks on Maine shores in the wintertime. All that therapy! All that conversation! I've been over this ground. Over it and over it and over it. I'm bored by it! Who are we anyway, we weary, middle-aged parents here in the room with our buddies dutifully sitting knee to knee? We're Boomers! We've done this! We've spent *years* wandering around inside our own heads, delving into every nook and cranny. This wandering may in fact be part of the reason our kids are in this place. We were so busy working out our own stuff that we didn't notice theirs.

Or something. I don't know.

We talk and we talk, we sit and we talk, when all we really want to do is to see our children. That's what we're here for. To see our children and to know that they are well.

The lights come slowly on. The walls are covered with bright posters. Things our kids drew after their Life Steps. Their

Life Step Promise, dredged out of the intensity of their experiential jag. I find Augusta's. "I am a passionate loving sister
who is alive with feeling."

They have made scrolls for us. Augusta's is bright colored
and painted beautifully. "Martha: I hope it went well. I will
see you soon. I hope you learned something valuable. I miss
you and my brother. I miss a lot of things. I want to go home.
Because I miss you. I love you. Augusta."

She has drawn Mount Desert Island. Its green spruce
trees. Its lavender mountains. Its blue sea. She has made little arrows pointing to the mountains, pointing to the sea:
"My island, which I miss," "My ocean, which I miss."

Next we split into our sections and they tell us about each of
the schools. We're in the Lower School. Rose takes our
group. She is enormous. We sit in a circle of folded chairs
and she tells us about the rules for our visit. She looks at the
ceiling while she's talking as if the rules were written on the
ceiling of the big room. We know most of it: no black
clothes, no rock music, no jewelry, no makeup. She tells us
how the kids bring drugs into the school in their shampoo, so
don't buy them shampoo. No candy. She tells us how to be-
have with our children. It's like she's giving us rules for how
to be with some strange animal, the care and feeding, for the
one day we will spend with our children. We never knew, it
turns out, what we were doing. They have to tell us.

We all have questions, but not about the program; mostly
our questions are about our own children. After the circle
disperses we are all ourselves like children, crowding around
Rose, trying to get in close. We all have the same question:

How's our girl? How is she? Don't worry, Rose, tells us. We will get to see our children tomorrow.

That night, after a long walk with my buddy and her ex-husband, I return to the Riverhouse exhausted. Too much emotion. Too much talk. Too much music. Too many people. I don't know where Ben went, but some of the other parents are in the lobby. They're going to dinner. They take me along. And we all eat pizza in Bend as if we were regular people. We talk a little about the Life Step. The men are skeptical, the women want to believe in it.

"It would be different," we say, "if we were fifteen. It would be different if it went on and on the way the Life Steps really do, for days. They don't let them sleep much; they keep at them. It's experiential."

We're learning the language. We want to tuck away our skepticism because if this doesn't work, then what?

That night in my room I'm tired. I think I can sleep but I'm getting this rash. It itches. I can't sleep. I have to take an antihistamine. Then I sleep. Like someone put a pillow over my head. That deep.

19

THIS IS THE DAY we go to see Augusta. It's misty and chilly in Oregon, later the sun will come out.

I am nervous about seeing Augusta. The last visit was so horrible, and I have had all these months to ruminate punctuated only by her sporadic phone calls full of tears and fury at me for putting her in the school. Will she even look at me when I get there?

The forest is tall and beautiful and cool in the September Sunday morning. The lake I pass looks perfect. I can imagine coming here on vacation to a lodge or something and thinking it serene.

I get to the school.

Here goes.

There are those tall outside wood steps that I remember from last summer. So long ago.

Right at the top on the deck in the watery new light I see Ben and my daughter. She is hunched over the way she hunches when she is nervous or shy. Her little shoulders tucked in, hair down around her face, hiding her expression.

"Hi, Martha," she calls out to me. She hasn't called me Mommy in a while.

She looks okay. The blotches and the lines have subsided, leaving only a smear on each cheek like makeup or like a glad rash.

"Hi, honey."

She won't let me kiss her. She doesn't want me to hug her. She backs off.

Ben's standing there like a dummy. Me too. We're too big for this place, too big to be her parents, this little, hunched-over person. We stand there, we awkward three, a mismatched, lumpy set. Other awkward families pass by. I know most of the parents from the seminar. Their children look, when you see them, immediately recognizable as the daughter or son of those two. Nobody, though, looks happy or comfortable or relaxed. This is no family picnic. This is no regular school.

It's not a nuthouse. It's not as I thought it might turn out—sharp shrieks from the other corridor, someone struggling and whisked away. Patrolling counselors with their implied threats, their weary, measured tread—not that. But it's not a regular school either. It's not some happy prep school on parents' weekend with everyone hugging hello! hello! and dragging their parents off by the hand to show them Look my dorm room! My friends! What I made in art class! My paper I got an A on! My teacher! My other teacher! The gym! No, not quite like that.

The kids are cleaned up for us. But we look nervous and sad. We're trying to be glad to see our children. The parents are trying to forget all the things screamed at us last time we talked with our children. Trying to forget the feeling of fear and futility. Trying to forget standing silent in the silent dawn of our houses, waiting in the hallway while the "escort" took our children away. And the children, who, after all, are still children, though the boys are hairy with adolescence and the girls look like women—the children are trying their hardest to remember all those same bad things. To remember why they hate their parents that they love.

Or that's maybe what we think.

I don't know.

I'm in a weird gelatinous dream.

"Let's go inside," I say to the two of them that I am hooked to. "I'm cold," I tell them.

So we all go in.

We go in past the dining room and we take off our shoes so we can go into the big living room with its sunken floor and very good Oriental rug and comfortable chairs.

"It's not usually like this," my daughter tells us. "It's never like this," she says.

She says, "They're just doing this for the parents."

We sit together in the chairs and I give her the package I brought her, wrapped up because everybody likes a present. And because I remember the Christmas when my parents, her grandparents, gave her a big expensive fancy doll that my mother had had specially made, but Augusta wouldn't even look at it. Wouldn't like it. Wouldn't cuddle it because it came unwrapped. My mother had foolishly thought it would be cute to put the big doll right under the tree waving out. "NO!" screamed little Augusta, maybe four at the time, already pretty certain of her needs, her wants, her desires. She screamed "NO!" when faced with this unwrapped item. And pushed it away and never, in fact, reconciled herself to that doll, who was dogged by her history, cursed by her origins. That doll never did become a favorite, though, like everything else that has ever passed through Augusta's hands, she has her still.

I had the sweater wrapped.

She opens it, excited and pleased but with that little snotty reservation that she has developed, her way of receiving gifts.

She is embarrassed.

I know everything about her.

The sweater comes out.

"This isn't what I wear," she tells me, unhappy because it's not furry or embroidered or black or velvet or anything. It's just a sweater with its little maroon line running around the neck. Plain.

"Thanks," she tells me then, seeing my face.

We talk awkwardly and then she and another girl go off to the cabin to get something. When she comes back she is wearing the sweater. "But I don't like it," she reminds me.

Oh, yes, I know.

Our meeting with Rose is at one. So we have, it turns out, a lot of time to sort of sit here. Lunch at noon, but, other than that, not much to do.

The other kids come in and out with their equally awkward parents. She calls out to the other kids, jumps up, gives them hugs.

Then the long door opens at the far end of the big room and Rose comes in. Augusta happens to be looking over there and her whole face shines with the sight of her mentor. Then she quickly closes it down. I've seen it, but I pretend not to. Not to see the radiance of her love.

Rose comes right over waving hello here and there, putting her hand on one girl's head, one boy's shoulder. You can see that they love her, that she is important here, this big woman with the big bunchy long skirt and the big green sweater and the flower behind her ear. I can see in that moment why she works here. What she gets from it. How it is.

She comes right over to Augusta. Gives her a kiss.

"Give me a kiss, hon," she tells Augusta.

Augusta kisses her on the cheek.

But when Rose goes away Augusta says, "I hate her. She's really scary."

I don't say anything.

I feel as if I know exactly what to say, to not say, to my daughter, for the first time in years. I can do it now, here in this safe place with rules and staff to back me up, but for how long could I sustain it? Being with Augusta is like being onstage. It's like giving a speech every second, or like being in tough negotiations where the wrong phrase, the slightest falter, the wrong word blurted when you should have just shut up, and you're out millions and millions of dollars. That's how it feels.

It is so weird.

So I get out the cards and the cribbage board that I brought here from Maine, and we play a rubber sitting in the comfortable chairs. Ben watches us as we play away, using all the little phrases we've developed over the years. "Fifteen two, fifteen four, that is all so shut the door." "Your crib." "Nada (goddam thing)." And she laughs when she gets a great hand and practically skunks me on the first game, but when she takes the cards to shuffle one time her sleeve falls back and I see that pink scar running up her arm and I feel a cold clench in the center of my belly and the whole room stills.

Later we take a little tour of the campus with Augusta. She shows us her cabin. It's odd being with her, the back-and-forth of her. One second she is chattering excitedly, telling us about something she's done, some friend, the next minute, under her breath, "I hate it here. When can I come home?

"I don't have any friends. They're not like us. They're all preppies. They're all rich."

"Not anymore, they're not," I tell her. "Not if they're paying for this place."

She grins at my little feeble joke and then she's off again jabbering away in her excited way about the stuff she has to get. "I don't have any clothes." She tells us the food "is terrible, but they'll probably give you something good today so you won't know." She says she doesn't have any friends, they're all snobs. Then someone comes along and she throws her arms around her and hugs her.

Her cabin is number four. There are three girls who share the cabin, but she tells us that the one she liked best left, and the other one she likes is "getting pulled" by Christmas.

"You don't know," she tells us. "Everybody's leaving. They lie and say that kids like it here. Everybody hates it. They're all getting pulled."

Her room is neat. Three girls in a room and it's neat.

Her stuff is neat. The stuffed animal I sent her on the bed. Her books lined up. The picture of the family taken on my father's birthday—I didn't know if she would rip it up or what—is on her bulletin board and a picture that she did herself. She shows me two paintings she made. They're very good. Trees. Sky. She has always liked to paint trees, and they always look real.

We have lunch at the big table in the sunny dining room with Becca and her parents. Augusta is happy and talkative and later lets me take her picture standing outside in the sun with another girl.

I am proud of her.

I love her.

Ben stands nearby, snaps a photo of me with Augusta. A piece of sun pierces the clouds and shines right down on us. It's so warm.

After lunch we meet with Rose in her office, another cabin, full of a jumble of pictures, paintings, photographs, and flowers in vases, and beads hanging down. There's a shawl flung over a chair and a big white dog in the corner.

"I want you to sit like this," she tells us.

We four sit face-to-face; Rose by Augusta, Ben by me, facing one another. Our knees are touching.

"Okay," she tells us. "Augusta's going to come clean. She's going to tell you about all the stuff she's done. Do you have your list?"

Augusta gets a folded-up square of lined paper out of her pocket of her jacket.

"Now?" She looks at Rose.

"Yeah."

Rose takes a big breath. "I want you to just listen. Don't say anything. You'll have a chance to speak later. Just listen to what Augusta has to tell you. This is hard for her. But this is what she needs to do."

It feels a little like secret code stuff. There are so many special rituals to remember: certain phrases, certain ways you have to sit. We're filled up with this sort of thing from the last two days. I've already broken out in a rash. Something itchy all up and down my arms. Starting on my legs.

Augusta reads from her paper.

This is what she has to tell us:

She's been smoking since she was twelve. She was up to two and a half packs a day when she left home.

She was smoking a lot of pot. She was stoned before school, between classes, after school.

She took mushrooms and acid.

She was sneaking out a lot, going to all-night parties.

She had adult friends she was getting stoned with, including the twenty-eight-year-old son of an old friend. The father of one of Jack's friends. A wealthy summer guy from Philadelphia.

She got her friend Alexis started with eating disorders.

She got Rain started smoking.

She was doing some drinking early on, but not much.

She was dealing pot.

She was dealing acid.

She snorted cocaine, smoked laced weed.

She stole money from me.

She was shoplifting.

She stole cars.

She got Jack stoned.

She made several suicide attempts—with pills, by cutting her wrists.

She fooled around with lots of guys, but she is still a virgin.

There's more.

She says all this stuff in a certain way without crying. She has her mouth fixed in that ironic expression she used to wear when she was berating me for being a terrible mother. I feel as if I've crept inside myself, deep inside of my shell of a body like a mouse in a teapot, deep inside, crawling up only to look out through the spout.

She's finished.

Rose, who has been watching Augusta the whole time, turns to us.

"Now how do you respond to this?" she asks us.

Ben tells her he's proud of her for telling us, but that he feels bad that she lied to us.

I know I'm supposed to say something. I thank her for being so honest. I say it was my job to keep her safe, and that I failed her.

"You didn't do this," she says fiercely. "It was my choice."

I tell her I love her. I tell her she's a powerful person.

"Hug your parents," says Rose, and finally, for the first time in months and months, my daughter hugs her father. And then she hugs me. I want to hold her forever. It feels so familiar. It feels like a dream. I can smell the way she smells. I put my face up against her and feel her little strong stubborn body just like a little pony, the way she's always felt.

20

WE'VE BEEN GRANTED an off-campus visit because we've done so well. We go to the nearby town, but there isn't all that much to do in Lyle on a Sunday afternoon in September. Augusta wants to go to the Dairy Queen, so we go to the Dairy Queen, and some of the others are there with their parents. The kids all order big fancy sundaes and Blizzards and milk shakes while the parents have coffee. All the kids bunch up together in a booth and laugh and eat their big fancy sundaes and eye the town kids, who eye them back.

And all the parents slump together in another booth dead eyed, stunned. All of us have been through the first session, the coming clean session, and we are all exhausted by emotion and revelation. We look at one another with odd lifeless sympathetic weariness, shipwrecked soldiers in the Dairy Queen.

"What do you want to do now?" I ask Augusta.

"We're supposed to be spending time together," she tells me. "Let's go for a walk," she says.

"All three of us?"

"Yeah, Mommy," she says patiently.

So we walk down the dusty streets of Lyle, a stretch of dilapidated town that is someone's home. Past the nice old city hall, past the dull shops closed for Sunday. Past the roads that turn off into neighborhoods of little Oregonian houses. We come to a sunny park with a swing set and a slide and jungle gym and a couple of picnic tables. Some of the other families turn up then, and the kids all climb around on the jungle gym and swing on the swings and even go down the slide. We take their pictures. They smile and wave. Augusta shows her letter from her brother to Becca, who gets a crush on him long distance. We take more photographs, we parents with our cheap disposable cameras.

Some of the men sit at one of the picnic tables in their good clothes chatting morosely. I walk away a little with Becca's mother, Roz, and we must seem to sort of stagger as we go, slanted against the slanted sunlight of the late afternoon.

We talk softly together, looking back once in a while at our daughters together high up on the top of the jungle gym to make sure, I guess, they don't run away, go steal cigarettes, go score some drugs, hitchhike off down the road out of Lyle and away forever.

"How bad was yours?" I ask Roz.

"Pretty bad. The only thing is, I was right. I wasn't imagining things. It was all going on. More."

"I know."

"I mean she's thirteen. She was having sex with her friends' parents. She was doing all kinds of drugs."

"I know."

I show Roz my rash. "What do you think this is? Do you think it's my sweater?"

"No, I've had that. I think you get it from this." She waves her arm at the park, at the town of Lyle, at the 7-Eleven across the road with its gaggle of teens with big pants going in and coming out, eyeing our children from across the street, our daughters on the jungle gym posing for photographs for their fathers.

"Let's see," she suggests, and I push up my sleeve and I show her my arms and the bumpety red rash all up and down.

"And it's on my neck, too, and it's on my legs."

"I don't know," she says. "I don't know."

Everybody wants dinner then, because we all have to get the kids back to the school by seven thirty, so we all troop down in our rental cars to Pioneer Wheel, a big family restaurant, and there the kids all want to sit together and order enormous soft drinks and huge dinners which they mostly don't eat and laugh and laugh and I find myself again sitting at the table with the adults and I almost make a scene, almost start crying. I want to be with my daughter! But one of the women tells me gently, "But this is how we have to do it now. We all feel that way." So I sit down anyway and eat my soup.

Ben keeps getting up to go out. He tells me he's sick so I wind up driving Augusta back to the school and then I go back to the hotel, but I can't sleep so I take allergy medicine and I surf through the channels and watch bits and pieces of TV Americana in my hotel room in Bend, where people come—people actually come here for vacations, come here on purpose—because it is, I suppose, it's beautiful, and I finally go to sleep.

The next day we get her for the whole day.

Ben goes over early to pick her up and the idea is that she

will spend half the day with me and half the day with him and we will meet in the middle for lunch.

It's colder and sunnier today and it gradually warms until it is one of those perfect September days and we are in perfection.

Augusta needs new clothes so today we will buy her clothes.

I have not spent this much time with my daughter since we drove to Portland together last March. I don't know how to do it. I don't know who she is anymore. I'm a little afraid of her. I know her completely. She feels like a stranger and like a piece of my own skin. I keep turning in the car to look at her. Her blue eyes. Her soft hair. Her face, which is like my face only it is her face and she is so young.

I want to pat her.

But I am afraid to touch her.

She seems endlessly dear to me. I am afraid she'll get mad. It is as delicate being with her, as prickly and dangerous and stilty, as a first date. She is my own daughter but we have been apart too long.

We go to a big outlet center and right away there are other kids and parents from the school all buying new pants, new belts. I need socks. She tries things on and asks me how she looks.

We walk from store to store in the still air.

Later in a nice old-fashioned department store we find great stuff—expensive faded overalls, too expensive but I buy then. I would buy her anything today. Anything, if she would just once more call me Mommy, just say, "Do you think I look fat, Mommy?" in the dressing room, turning from the mirror to look at me, to show me my own girl standing in her faded expensive overalls caring what I think.

"Do you need more underwear?" I ask her. "Do you need pajamas?"

In downtown Bend we go into a hip chic expensive shop and look at shadowy clothes hung in racks. I was here last summer, when I visited the school. I loved the clothes in here. They looked like clothes I'd buy. Now here we are looking at them together. It's like when we used to sit on the green couch and look at catalogues.

"What do you think?" I ask her, holding out a beigey linen skirt.

"For you," she tells me. "Not for me."

"No, not for you. You think I'm crazy?"

It's our chorus. It's our ritual.

She touches the velvet shirts, the chenille for fall.

"I love this stuff," she says.

"I know."

I do know. I know what she loves. She loves velvet. She loves kittens. She loves furry things, glittery things, she loves old sixties hippie things. She loves me.

Later we meet Ben on the corner. He looks terrible. While she's picking out her sandwich in a restaurant he tells me that he was in the hospital last night. "There's something wrong," he says. "It's all this stress."

He looks awful. His face is the wrong color. His hair is awry.

"What is it?"

"Something with my stomach," he tells me. "It's too hard, seeing her here. I had some blood."

"What did the doctor say?"

"He told me to take Pepto-Bismol. He gave me all these tests. He says it's stress. I don't know if I can do much. I might go back today, drive back to Portland. Can you get her back to the school?"

"Sure. Are you okay?"

He's not okay. I think now that he might be really sick. This might be how I remember the beginning, when I found out he was really sick. He seems dear to me, too, now. We're in this together, this odd boat.

It's gotten warmer, so we go to the little park by the river, and Augusta eats her lunch from the hippie restaurant and we all sit on the grass together. She gives me part of her sandwich. Ben doesn't want anything, just some water.

"Daddy doesn't feel very good," I tell Augusta.

She continues eating.

"He's thinking about going back today," I tell her. "I can take you back to school."

She says, "Okay, can I still get my Birks?"

He was going to buy her new Birkenstocks. That's what she wants. New ones.

"Sure."

They go off to buy her shoes, and I hang around in the sunny park until they return and Ben tells her he's going back to Portland. When he hugs her good-bye, he is crying.

"God," she says when she gets in the car with me. "He was crying."

"He loves you," I tell her. "This is hard for him."

"Then why do you make me stay here," she asks me, "if it's so hard?"

Beats me, I think. I think I'd like to take her home with me. She seems so good. She seems so healthy and kind now, and so clean. But then I think that it's the school that has made her this way and I wonder how much better she can get if she stays. And she seems resigned to it, even with the steady drumbeat of her complaints, her insistence that she has no friends there, that she wants to leave, to come home.

She seems happier and healthier than I've seen her in years. She is kinder, more my daughter.

We go to a huge Barnes & Noble and look at books for a while. I wonder what I'll do if she tries to run away. They have warned us to watch the kids. Don't let them go to the bathroom alone. Don't let them be out of your sight. But I let her be out of my sight in the long rows of books because I think that she will not leave me now.

I lose her for a moment in the fiction section. And in that moment I feel a bubble of fierce pride for her indomitable spirit at the same time that I feel disaster and fear. I have started to panic, searching up and down the aisles, when I find her sitting cross-legged on the floor by the music books reading the lyrics to songs she loves, just reading the lyrics, sitting on the floor.

Swirling in my head are stolen cars, cigarettes at twelve, eleven even. Acid. Mushrooms. Grass. I knew it and I didn't know it. Maybe I should look in the parenting section. I did that once, last spring, went to Borders in Bangor and looked at the parenting books. Okay, tell me, so what do I do now? But the cases were so much milder. They only talked about little problems. When your child begins to show different patterns—changes in eating patterns, changes in sleeping patterns, depression, mood swings, schoolwork slipping—choose one. Mark boxes. How about when your child does *everything?* How about when the whole child collapses? How about when everything is wrong all the time and she is screaming at you and threatening you with a knife and you are crying and she is crying and it feels like the end of your life? Where's the book for that? Where's the book for my life's in a shambles? My daughter hates me? Is there a special section or is it under self-help? Inspirational? Health? Science fiction? Beats me.

We call her brother in Maine from the pay phone by the rest rooms. She looks so pretty standing talking into the phone that I have to take her picture. "Mom," she says, but she doesn't really mind. She loves her brother and she is so happy to be talking to him again. She chatters with him about the school, about certain of her friends, wants the gossip. "Yes, I told her everything, I told her," she says and looks around at me.

I feel like a fat guard standing there by the rest rooms as the people go in and out of the swinging doors, standing there watching my daughter talking to her brother in Maine. What a family.

The phone call's over. "Write me!" she calls to him across the miles. "Send me your picture! Send me a good picture! Without your hat!" She laughs and hangs up and is still smiling as we walk out of the store.

It's time to go back, she reminds me.

"I don't want to be late," she tells me. "My agreement says I have to be back by seven thirty."

"Are you hungry?" I ask her. "Do you want to stop for anything? Dairy Queen?"

"No."

She wants to get back, and as we drive back the long way between the fields and farms with the mountains all around ringing the horizon, we both know it's time for her to go back. It's odd. It doesn't feel anything. Not sad or worrisome or awkward anymore. It just feels like it's time for her to be getting back.

When I take her there the other kids are already coming in with their parents, too. They have to be strip-searched. She submits to this as if it were normal. Shows all the things she bought—empties out the bags of clothes, shows what she's got.

The staff member on duty admires the clothes, even as she efficiently checks pockets and sleeves for hidden contraband. "Oh, I like that," she tells Augusta. And, "Are you sure that shirt's long enough to tuck in?"

We go into the library and I get to hug her one more time.

"I love you, honey," I tell her. She is so short and she has such soft hair. I hug her tight and she lets me. Doesn't pull away from me. Doesn't hate me.

I pat her one more time and then it's time and I go.

When I start back toward Portland in my rented car it's late in the day. The sun will be setting as I drive back. The sunset will be beautiful and the whole sky will turn many colors. I decide I won't cry, turn on Public Radio, and drive away.

21

"She's better," I tell everyone.

It is a magic week. When I get back I am buoyed by rightness and busyness. I was right to send her there. It was the right thing. She is healthier. She is better. She called me Mommy. She let me hug her. She was nice.

I'm so excited. Maybe she's going to be all right. I'm full of energy. I throw myself into our radio station's next big promotion. Imus is coming back to Bangor on October 9 for a national broadcast from the Bangor Civic Center. He's the morning show on one of our radio stations. And he likes things just so, and I want everything to be perfect, so I have to personally make sure that the hotel rooms are perfect, and that there are enough chairs in the Civic Center, and the sound's working and the tickets are sold, and the spots are running, and the sponsor breakfast is catered, and the screens for MSNBC are up, and the press has kits, and the limos are hired, and the private plane is met, and all the staff who need to spend the night have rooms at the Holiday Inn, and there are reservations at the Seadog for the whole crowd for supper the night before. It's a big deal.

There's a lot to do and I am busy busy busy but I write to her and I tell her how much I love her and how proud I am, etc. I am really happy. She's going to be all right. I feel lighter than I have in months. Light.

But a week later, late at night, there's a call from the school. The sound of the phone wakes me up. Jack comes into my room. "It's the school."

I take the call. Augusta has run away. She's gone.

Six kids left together. "They should be easy to find. Staff is driving around, looking. The police have been notified. We'll find them."

And by next morning, sure enough, four of the kids have been returned to the school. But there are two girls still out. And one of them is Augusta.

The other girl, Nina, has run away a lot. In fact she was the one who ran away right before the parent seminar a week ago. They brought her back, and her parents were there, two grim-faced Mexican Americans with their old mother and their little coats against the chill of northern air. They came from southern California. Maybe the girls have gone back that way.

Now what?

We call back and forth. There's nothing. I don't want to tell my parents. I don't want to tell Jack. I tell Ben over the phone that night, and more as they tell me more. Every time he cries. And what do I do? I go to work earlier and earlier. I get up in the morning. I work at my desk. I take my walk. I go to work.

One morning early I am taking my walk up Schoolhouse Ledge. She's been gone four days now. It's foggy and the road is damp. The summerhouses are empty and the woods look quiet. I don't hear any birds. I walk up the hill fast, right to the top, and stand on a rock looking out at the mountains, or what I can see of the mountains, half hidden in the fog.

I don't cry. I just sort of clench up. I clench up and once in a while something happens and it hits me again, hard. That my daughter is missing. I just sort of clench up my face in a kind of a grimace that would probably appear comical if someone happened to pass me when I was making that face, if I was walking and by accident let my mind wander out of its careful grooves, and by accident I touched the hot deep center of the pain.

Every day the headline in my head is *Still Missing*.

I don't tell my parents. Not yet.

I am in touch with the other girl's parents. They have some leads. Nina made a call to her old boyfriend and told him she was in California.

Is she still with Augusta? We don't know.

I don't tell Jack.

Ben and I talk on the phone late at night when neither of us can sleep. He says his body is breaking up under the stress. His blood pressure, he says, is sky high. His stomach a wreck.

I remember the first time Augusta was missing overnight. It was the September night a year ago when she and her brother and Danny Michaud's stepson took his grandfather's truck and drove all over the Island smoking cigarettes and dope and careering through back roads to escape our dogged pursuit in Danny's big old-fashioned fancy car. Alton and Jack got home, but Augusta was afraid to come home so she stayed out all night. I'm still not sure where. She told me later that she spent the night on the golf course, that she heard us looking for her later with the police. But I'm not sure she was telling me the truth. She was gone all night. We searched until about 2 A.M. and then finally went home and went to bed without her. I remember when I was in the house after we had given up the search, I remember turning the heat up so it would be warmer in the house because it was cold outside and foggy and I thought how cold she must be out there. That's the way I've felt this week too with Augusta gone. It must be cold out there. When I see the rain sheeting down outside the windows and the black trees banged about by the wind, it must be cold out there, and up goes the heat. Even though this rain is here in Maine and her rain is where? California? Oregon? Nevada? I don't know. Still, the sight of it makes me turn up the heat to keep my daughter warm.

During the worst of it I could always hear her little voice. She would be at the table with us glaring at me, not eating, furious over something, and it was as if I could hear her little voice Mommy Mommy. And now that she is missing I can sometimes hear that little voice. It's the voice of her youngest self. And I hear it when there's nothing I can do.

Why are they like this? Any of them? I have gone through her childhood until I am sick of it—all my misdeeds, all my failings as a mother. How I got angry. How I did or didn't do the right thing. What her father did. The school. What if I hadn't let her? Why didn't I stop it? But then everything along the way seems inevitable and she herself seems inevitable. Often I have thought what I would do if she were dead. What I would say at her funeral. I would blame every-

218

one—the school for abandoning her, her friends for giving her drugs, everyone who watched her and didn't do anything—and I would save the biggest blame, the harshest judgment, for myself.

I am, amazingly, continuing to go to work. Every day. Organizing the Imus remote. Being interviewed on television. Making reservations at the hotel. Setting up the big staff dinner.

I sit at my nice desk all neat and tidy with my lists of things to do—all my careful lists of slightly unpleasant or dull or scary chores and little rewards in the evening—ordering something out of a catalogue, something that will transform this dreary October landscape with its slashing skies and windy rain-swept trees and wild patches of unmelted snow—transform it into yes a summer afternoon with light light linen clothes in colors that seem like inspiration: butter, straw, sage, wheat.

I'd be good at making up the names of colors for the catalogues. I would invent better names than aubergine. I'd make up names more evocative than the names from those distant perfect catalogue worlds, names like Orb, Sunlit, Dreamscape, Lunar. How about Dried Menstrual Blood? Spoiled Clementine. Bathtub Mold. Midnight Vomit. Sorrow. Grief (a sharper yellow) and the fashionable, dismal, faded gray of Despair.

I'd invent words that have never been used for colors before. I'd invent words that would be understood by the women who lie on their couches in the evening with their stacks of catalogues, who roam the Web looking at pictures of things that they might buy. They wouldn't even need swatches. These are colors they would recognize. Heartbreak. Divorce. Terror. Missing Child.

✦

Maybe she's in San Francisco.

I lived in San Francisco thirty years ago fresh from Antioch College on my first co-op job. Shared an apartment with some other Antioch students in an area we found out was called the Tenderloin. Late at night we'd hear gunshots, in the elevator we'd see shriveled drag queens and the odd-shaped faces of the other residents, the shuffling bums. There were five of us in that two-bedroom apartment for one month. We pushed the beds together and all slept in a heap, as I recall. Meltzer. Martin Gottlieb. Tim from St. Louis. Sally from Peoria. And me.

My mother had no idea.

I was seventeen.

I had a job. I was enrolled in college, so I must be safe.

Later we moved to the Haight and lived on Oak Street on the Panhandle.

San Francisco, 1969. We had the top floor of one of those tall old wooden town houses. When we moved in there were already some other tenants there. They never left. The old man with the white beard who lay on the green velvet couch all day and drank wine and smoked Benson & Hedges. There was a tall man who was blind in one eye and who read the Bible over and over at the kitchen table. The one with the baby. The man named Mother. Prince Honey Vibes. They all stayed on. We Antioch kids worked at our various jobs and lived in the apartment and figured we were finding out about Life. Haight Street on a Sunday afternoon. Dog shit and Indian bell-bottoms. Be-ins in the Park all afternoon. The waft of incense and of marijuana. Someone getting high. The dark cold rain.

So now my own daughter is probably in San Francisco. My mother used to wait for my letters to know that I was safe. The mailman, she told me later, used to call her at work. "You got one!" I didn't even know his name, but my mother always knew everyone. Knew their names, knew all about their children. Told them about her children. Knew when their wives were sick. Knew what they made. My amazing mother whom I used to hate.

And now it's my turn. Now my daughter hates me. Runs away. Doesn't call to tell me. Doesn't write a letter.

No mailman here, not in these thrifty times. Not when mail has been reduced to bills and catalogues for the women on their couches, to notices and pleas for contributions. To the library. To the other library. To the children's museum that they want to build in downtown Bangor. Get the kids off the street.

She's still missing.

The school says they can't do anything. They say they're there for me.

Big deal.

The other girl's father hires a detective. Nina has taken some money out of an ATM machine in San Francisco.

My sister has contacted every hot line in America.

She has a friend in San Francisco who is walking up and down the streets with a photograph of Augusta.

Her friend goes to the shelters. "Have you seen this girl?"

She goes to the soup kitchens.

She goes up and down the streets of San Francisco.

Her closest thing to success is the first day out. The first evening she spots two girls in a doorway scoring some drugs. She goes over to them. "Are you Augusta?" she asks the one with the blue eyes.

"No. I'm Lily," the girl answers.

"Are you from Maine?"

"New York," my daughter answers and she runs away.

My sister faxes me reams of papers to fill in, information about my daughter, and things to sign and fax back.

I am supposed to go to Seattle for a radio convention next Wednesday. I'm supposed to meet with my broker. Meet with the fellow who might buy the stations. Go to seminars and big buffets.

I get up every morning.

I have broken out anew in my rash.

The night before the Imus broadcast, from my hotel room in Bangor, I call the Head of the school and we talk. Augusta has been missing five days. We think she is still alive. We think she is in San Francisco.

"Call her friends," the Head tells me. "Call all her friends and get them to call you if they hear anything. Maybe she'll call them. Maybe she'll call you. Hang in there."

I start calling. Every time I speak to someone new I start to cry.

"If you hear from her," I tell them, "please just ask her to call me. Tell her I'm not mad. I just want to know that she's all right."

I call Bill and get his wife, Sally. She says she would like to ask some Carmelite nuns to pray for Augusta's safety. I don't know what she's talking about. I tell her go ahead. She says she's been so worried ever since Bill told her. "I wanted to call you," she says, "but I didn't know if I should."

"Sure," I tell her, "you should always call. You should always reach out. It doesn't matter what you say. It's just so lonely when you're going through something like this."

So then she wants to know, like I'm the oracle, if she should call the girl who has the brain tumor at the school or maybe her parents. And here I am advising her. Call her, I say, it doesn't matter what you say. And in this way I suppose I'm learning some life lessons. I try to think this is faith at work, or something that moves this out of the realm of pain and into the useful, worthy realm of good growth or some damn thing. But mostly I don't care about all this. I am impatient with the plod of events and the world. I am impatient with the intentions, good and bad, and worries over such tiny matters. I just want Augusta to be safe. I just want Augusta to be well.

I call her friend Daisy, who used to ride around with my daughter in her red car with the top down on triumphant spring days—two teenage girls stoned and beautiful waving out of the open car at everyone on the streets of Bar Harbor. I call her up and when I try to tell her what is happening I can't help it, I start crying in my hotel room in Bangor. I worry at the same time that I sound a little crazy. Tears are so inappropriate and so pitiful when you're not young. And I don't want to scare her but I want her to understand at the same time the intensity of my plea. And she promises she'll let me know if Augusta calls her.

"I will," she says. "I promise."

I call the policeman's wife and she says she feels terrible for me but I can tell that she can't wait to get off the phone.

I have cancer, I guess. I have some bad disease that they might catch—the healthy ones, the happy ones, the ones confounded by simple problems: Oh God how am I going to get it all done? The cat needs to go to the vet, the back door screen's broken, and I've got an appointment at the dentist in fifteen minutes! I want that too but instead I have this. What do they think, if they brush up against me they'll catch it?

🌀

The Imus broadcast is a big success. The night before I treat my staff to dinner at the Seadog. We're all hilarious. Some of us have worked together for fifteen years. We've got our jokes. We're almost siblings. No one knows.

At 4 A.M. we're on our way through the dark dawn to the Civic Center. A crowd already at the door. They call to us as we go by.

"When are you opening the doors?" they ask us. They can't wait to see him.

And then it starts to get really busy, and I welcome the busyness. Taking tickets. Keeping people out of the chosen seats. My tall son ushering the sponsors to their front-row seats. Making sure the TV people have what they need. Listening to the audience laugh and laugh.

"Isn't this great?" we tell one another. "Isn't this great?"

The money's all going to a certain charity. A home for teenagers in Bangor. Kids that haven't done so well, couldn't get along with their families. Took drugs. Dropped out of school. It's in an old house. The kids help with the chores. They go to school. They have jobs. It's a good place and they need the money and I picked it out.

I'm wearing one of my suits. I'm like the hostess. I'm on TV. I'm in charge. I haven't slept. Under the sleeves of my suit jacket my rash is brutal. But it doesn't show and nobody knows it's there.

🌀

It's been six days now. I have to tell Jack.

I call him into the living room after the broadcast and the light in the living room is different than it's ever been. Is it the afternoon? Is it Saturday morning? The room is very quiet and the walls, which are pinky orange, look gray and still.

I tell him first, "I have to tell you something," so he'll know it's something bad.

That's how we do things.

"I have to tell you something. Augusta ran away from school."

He looks at me.

"She left last Sunday. I didn't want to tell you because I thought they'd find her, but they haven't found her and she's still missing. She's with another girl. They think they're in San Francisco."

He still looks at me. "I knew she'd run away," he tells me.

He tells me, "I told you."

I don't say anything.

I want him to know this is a big deal. I want him to know how scared and sad I am so he'll be kind, so he'll understand the enormity of the situation. But I don't want to scare him too much.

"I'm worried," I tell him.

"What are you going to do?" he asks me.

"I don't know. Pray."

We don't talk much more about it. He's only fourteen, after all. Above all he doesn't want me to start crying and he's scared I might.

I want to, but I'm still clenched. The tears come abruptly and without warning these days and they jump out of my face like gravel.

❦

Now that everybody else knows I have to tell my parents before they hear it someplace. Before someone mentions it to them like they already know.

I drive the long drive down to their house. I called them first, to make sure they'll be there. They're so busy. Busy with my father's heart. Busy with my mother's boards and committees. Busy with dinner parties. But I have to tell them, so I call them up and tell them I need to talk to them about something.

They are curious and delighted. They think the sale might have gone through. They think I might be telling them I'm getting married. They think lots of things but they don't think of what I have to tell them.

It's gray again. This is fall. On the drive down, even with the heat on, my car's cold. The sky looks cold. The sea doesn't sparkle. A lot of the leaves are down and where the leaves aren't down they might as well be. The ground's wet and the road's dirty.

"Do you want some tea?" my mother asks.

"No thanks."

We're in the room they call the morning room. They sit together on the couch, look at me expectantly. My mother just came in from getting some wood from outside. When she takes her hat off her hair's all sticking up, which makes me not want to tell her. She looks exhausted already. Exhausted by my father's illness. Exhausted still by my own teenage shenanigans. Just wait.

"I got a phone call from the school. Augusta's missing."

They look at me.

"She ran away last Sunday. I didn't want to tell you but I have to tell you."

I spend the rest of the weekend cleaning house. I have started a project of cleaning out the attic. Stuffed with the stuff of years. Old clothes. Photographs. Books from when the children were little. Every *Highlights* magazine ever received. All their schoolwork. I don't have to keep it all. I am trying to get rid of some of this stuff but it's hard. Each photograph I throw out I feel like I'm throwing away my children. All their old clothes. Little shirts they wore. Each event. I can hardly stand it. Old stuffed animals. Their little shoes.

I have to do it. I have to do something. So I spend a chilly day in the attic bagging stuff up, hauling bags out to the car, driving them down to the Dumpster by the dock.

If I fill up ten bags full of junk and get rid of them I will get a prize.

If Augusta is found and is safe I will get a prize.

But she's still missing.

It's Jack's birthday. Now he's fifteen. It rains all day. I've invited the parents to dinner and they drive up.

I make a nice supper and we all sit around the table and watch Jack open his presents. Everything's great.

It's been eight days since Augusta left the school.

I get a call from Will, the enormous detective who "escorts" kids hither and thither. I spoke to him last summer about possibly coming to get Augusta, but he wanted $7,000 for the trip east to get her and to take her and it cost too much. Now the other girl's father is paying him to track the girls down and bring them back to Forest Ridge. It's like they're outlaws. It's so dramatic, like some movie. The school keeps telling me don't worry. Will can find them. Don't worry about the money. It's been taken care of. The other girl's father can afford it. It turns out later, I find out weeks later, that Nina is eighteen and her father is afraid I'm going to sue him. Last thing on my mind. All I want is a phone call telling me my daughter is okay.

Two days later Will calls me from a car telling me he is about to get her.

He calls me later from a hotel. He has my daughter.

"She's really hungry," he tells me. "She's all right," he tells me. "She's eating."

I ask him stupidly who should I pay and again he tells me not to worry.

I have to call everybody. I have to tell Jack and my parents. I have to call my sister. I have to talk to the school. Rose says, I knew he'd find her. The Head says she's going to have to do some real work now. She's going to have to prove to us that she's ready to come back to Forest Ridge. It's decided that right now she will go to the Wilderness Program in Idaho, where she was last summer. Will can take her. Don't worry about the money, they keep telling me.

I feel like I'm sending her to jail, sending her back into the Wilderness. Isn't Idaho cold now? In the fall? Isn't it cold out there? I don't know what else to do. Everything's so rushed.

It's the middle of the night. I have to go down to the police station to use their fax machine to fax permission to someone to take her somewhere, someone to drive her, someone to put her into the Wilderness Program, someone to give her a medical checkup.

I'm supposed to leave for Seattle the next morning for a big radio convention. I'm meeting out there with my broker, and with the head of the company that might buy the radio stations. I'm all packed. I can sleep on the plane.

There are a million things to remember. I have to hurry.

And then, all of a sudden, it's a cold gray morning and I'm on the plane headed out of Bangor and I realize that in all that hurrying, in all those phone calls, in all those arrangements and permissions, I never even spoke to her at all.

22

FROM MY HOTEL ROOM in rainy Seattle I speak to the woman at the "safe house" where Augusta's staying for $350 a night. They will take her to the program the next day (transport, $325). None of it has any meaning. I've already FedExed the check. I finally ask if I can speak to her but they say no, not now, it's better if you don't.

"She's fine," the woman tells me. "She's watching television."

So instead I speak compulsively to everybody connected with her in any way—to the parents of the other girl. To the man who took her there. To the people at the Wilderness Program. I tell them to watch out. That the last time she was there she cut her wrists. Don't give her a knife, I tell them. Watch her, I say. I want to talk to everyone. I want to go there and put my arms around her. I want to go there and keep everyone off her. I want to hug her. I don't want to see her. I don't even know if I know her. I don't even know if she's sane.

And I don't get to speak to her for three weeks.

I do write her a letter, which they assure me she will get to read during her "solo" on the desert.

Sitting in my office home in Maine. I write: I'm so glad you're safe.

She writes me back an angry letter, which they fax to me. "I'm always safe," she tells me. "I can take care of myself."

There is one phone call and she just yells.

The school isn't sure they want her back. I have to talk them into it. Is it because I'm not paying full tuition or do they know something I don't know?

They say they think maybe she ought to be somewhere else. Somewhere, they say, "restricted." Like a jail?

All the time I'm at work. We're negotiating the sale of the radio stations, but nobody knows about it and it might not even happen, so I'm still planning the New Year's Eve dance party at the Ellsworth Holiday Inn. I'm hiring a disgruntled ex-salesperson who worked here years ago, then worked for somebody else, now might come back. She wants way too much money.

But I have this little edge when I'm negotiating all these things. I don't care. They tell you, when you're learning about business, that you shouldn't care too much. But I *really* don't care. Three million. Four million. So what. Four hundred. Six hundred. Fine. I don't care who pays for the paper tablecloths that will be soggy with cheap spilled champagne fifteen minutes into the new year. They pay. We pay. Okay with me. I'm winning everything. It's amazing. I should have done this years ago. Had cancer.

Augusta's at the Wilderness camp for three weeks this time. I'm on the phone with the Head of the School trying to talk her into taking Augusta back. I'm on the phone with my education consultant, who says she'll talk to the school. I'm on the phone with Rose, who is inexplicably scrubbing pots noisily the whole time we're talking, and I imagine her in a battered West Coast kitchen in some funky hippie seventies abode in her big skirt scrubbing away while we talk. She sighs and says, still scrubbing, that she'll fight to get Augusta back in.

"I specialize in tough cases," she tells me. "I'll go get her myself, if I have to," she says.

I want to trust her, I want to think that she will save Augusta, this enormous woman, but I don't know if she's really gifted, a wonderful counselor, a magician, a sage, or just some lumpy weird one with no life. She's all I've got. She's the one who tells me she can save my daughter.

I speak with Augusta's "field supervisor" in the Wilderness, who tells me one week that Augusta is "really negative," "not buying in," "furious," "self-pitying." The works. But the next week she says that Augusta has had a really good week, is being a leader, helping other kids. I grab at this one.

"That's how she is," I tell this woman I will never meet, somewhere in Idaho. "She's really compassionate. She's very charismatic."

I don't know if she's charismatic. I don't know if she's crazy. They're hinting that she might be crazy. I don't know.

One night Nina's mother calls from California. She's the girl Augusta ran away with. Nina's staying home, her mother tells me.

"You would not believe the things they did to her at that school."

The mother tells me that they scream at the kids. That they told Nina she was a slut. She asks if I would like to speak with Nina.

Nina gets on the phone. Her voice is light and high. I try

to picture her. I only met her once. She looked so tiny. Dark eyed. Dangerous. Disturbed. But on the phone she sounds only young.

"No, I'm not going back there," she tells me in her little voice. "I'm doing really good."

I tell her I hope she takes good care. I pretend I'm talking to my own daughter who will not talk to me.

The school says they don't want her. They want her in a lockup. That's what they do. If Forest Ridge doesn't work. There's always someplace else.

But then the Head has a phone call with Augusta and Augusta says she's ready to go back. That she'll try harder. That she'll be good.

So they relent after the three weeks and she goes back. We have our first conference call together and I am supposed to tell her how I felt when she was missing, with Ben and some stupid staff counselor who doesn't know the right things to say. Who has been told what to say but keeps getting it wrong. Rose is on vacation. So we get this one instead. This lummox. We want Rose. She knows what to say.

"So," he says, the way they teach them, "tell Augusta how it was for you when she was missing."

I go first because Ben always makes me go first.

But it's not the way Rose does it, and we're all uneasy and I get it wrong and sound too harsh telling her how sad and scared I was; how I thought she was dead. How I cried, how sad Daddy was. I tell her about walking up Schoolhouse Ledge and saying her eulogy, about telling her friends, about how it was for us when she was gone.

Augusta cries and says she doesn't care. She says we

kicked her out, that we don't care about her. She says we didn't write to her. She says she didn't call because she didn't want to get caught. She says she has dreadlocks and she has to get her hair cut. Her voice gets higher and she starts speaking faster. She's going to run away again first chance she gets. She wanted to cut her wrists again when she was in the car being escorted back from Wilderness to Forest Ridge. She would have cut her wrists, but she didn't have a knife, she says. She would have. She doesn't want to talk anymore. She hates us. She wants to go home.

They're watching her, they assure us. Watching her.

One of the kids is assigned to follow her around. The staff will keep their eye on her. She's safe.

I'll go out in December and see her at the next parent seminar. If she's still there.

I might sell the stations quicker than I think. Then what? What will I do then?

I want to feel normal again.

I want to just be in my house and go on a hike and go home and read on my bed in the late afternoon and have the children there with me, young again, when they still loved me. Was it ever like that? Some Hallmark card of a life? I don't remember.

I want to get rid of stuff. Out of Augusta's room. My own junk. My desk. The books that I don't read. The bathroom towels.

Anything I don't use or need. Get rid of it! Old clothes! Boxes of stuff! Letters from college! Get it out.

I want to be free to move around!

I came here with only a knapsack and a typewriter twenty-four years ago.

And look at all I've accumulated—a house! piles of clothing! two children! an ex-husband! books! boxes of letters! dishes! tiny shampoos from fancy hotels! vases! canned goods! jewelry! computers! acres of old journals! couches! bedsteads! toys galore! stuffed animals! and heaps of memories like wet rags, bunches of them, hanging off me, weighing me down.

I want to rise up, weightless and triumphant. I want to move unencumbered. The walking. The running. The escape.

How come she gets to run away? I want to. I want to run away. Out of my house, out of my towering, choking stuff swallowing me up in its dusty maw. Out of my own skin even. Out of my life with its restrictions and regrets and resistance. I want to run away, too. I want to run away—directionless, hatless, coatless—without a bag or even the knapsack that I brought a quarter-century ago when I came here to Maine.

I am going to see her in December and Jack is coming with me. Ben is going. We are all going. It turns out we are all going on the same plane—across the country all together, a ragged little band, her family.

I remember when she was younger, eight or nine, and we were having supper at the Colonel's Deli downtown, Augusta, Jack, and I. We used to go there often. I would bring whatever book we were reading and read to them quietly at the table while they drew on the paper place mats and we waited for our food. Pepperoni pizza. Cole slaw. Onion rings. Fish chowder. Grilled cheese sandwich. White bread and a pickle.

We liked it there. We went off-season—in the spring, when it had opened and it all felt new, and in the cold fall, when it stayed open after Labor Day and all the summer people had left except the old ones. We got a back booth and we read there and we had our meal. The little three of us.

This time Augusta had on her considering look. "I wish we were a normal family," she told us. "You know, a mother and a father and a sister and a brother. Maybe you should get married, Mommy."

"Marry who?" I asked.

Did she really want me to marry Thomas, my boyfriend then, with his shabby house, his odd poetic silences, his bony face?

"No, I guess not," she said. "And anyway, if you were married, then we'd have to wear those certain kind of hats. And I'd have to wear little dresses and Jack would have to wear a tie."

Always there was a hunger. Stronger than I realized. To be like other kids, or how she imagined other kids. Their normal lives. Their balanced families. Their TV dreams.

Augusta is not doing well at school. She is angry and surly, they tell me, and won't participate. Again, there is talk about not keeping her there—that she ought to go somewhere tougher, somewhere harder. In spite of all the evidence I keep wanting to believe it isn't really so bad. It can't be.

They say she feels as if nobody loves her.

Will she ever get better? I need to pray hard.

I have to balance everything. Not let anything show. Then

at one early-morning Rotary board meeting in Bangor, I let it slip. I'm at a table with people who have become my friends, meeting here 7 A.M. month after month discussing the business of Rotary. This morning we are discussing one of our members who hasn't paid his dues. He's been sick, somebody says, maybe he just forgot.

But people have to pay their dues to stay in Rotary. He's had reminders.

Then I speak up. I can't believe I'm saying this. We're all eating blueberry muffins. And I say, "Maybe you don't know, but I've been through a pretty horrific year myself this year, and I forgot my Internet access payment. I always pay my bills right on time, sometimes early. But I just forgot about it."

I stop then, like that explains it, what I mean, but they all just stare at me like sheep.

Then I'm embarrassed. I'm almost crying. If someone had put their hand over my hand lying on the table just then, I would have cried, but instead they all look aside and talk about other things. They don't know what I'm talking about. They're embarrassed for me. This isn't, after all, a group therapy session. This is a board meeting. This is not the place.

I try to remember that, but sometimes, through this long year, I've tempted to just blurt it out. Tempted, at Rotary, when it's time for Happy and Sad Dollars, when people take turns getting up waving their dollar bills and announcing they're giving a Happy Dollar because their son graduated high school with high honors, but a Sad Dollar because he got into Colby (and guess who's paying!). Happy Dollar for their daughter's wedding. Happy Dollar for their seventh grandchild. Happy Dollar for their thirty-fifth wedding anniversary. I've thought about it, sometimes, then, standing up. Giving a Happy Dollar myself. My daughter is alive. Sad Dollar: they say she might be crazy.

❀

While I'm at work, an old friend calls to talk about Jack. He's doing better, now that he's in the Alternative School. I know I should be happy, but I can hardly discuss it. I just feel too sad.

Instead, I talk about Augusta. My friend says they should check Augusta out for physical causes. He says that his own sister died of heroin. He tells me about going to a psychiatrist to talk about his sister. He asked the doctor what had happened to make his sister that way and the doctor told him, "Oh, you want the magic key! There's no magic key. It took a long time for your sister to get that way and it will take a long time to get her well."

He says you can't blame yourself or go over and over what happened. You just have to do your best. You want a reason so it's like an equation and you can change one variable and have it come out all right.

After I get off the phone I have to go over to the county courthouse to meet with the county commissioners. It's right next door. We're negotiating the renewal of our lease. We have some satellite dishes on the roof over there and I want to hand it over to the buyers with a clean lease. I've been crying, but no one can tell.

The meeting room is old and wooden. The men are very kind. They like me because I always make jokes and it must get a little dull over there in the county courthouse sometimes.

I have to sit through some other discussions. That's okay. It's already December. People have begun exchanging Christmas presents. My eyes are drawn to a cookie tin on one of the desks. It is decorated with snow-land scenes—a barn and a yellow house, some trees, some children, a snowy wooden fence, a sled. All bundled up, all Laura Ingalls Wilder, all snug. I want to go there. I want to live on that happy tin, delivered of all the sorrows, the sad scales of living, the dark alleyways, the angry daughters. Go to that world where the snow is so white.

I'm getting Christmas presents to take out to her. A blue fuzzy sweater that I hope she'll like. A couple of books. A new journal. "You always give me a journal," she always says. We're going out to see Augusta.

But then something happens.

The phone's in Jack's room. The call comes in the middle of the night. I don't even hear the phone ring, or if I do, I hear it in my dream. I don't wake up until my son's standing in my bedroom door.

"It's the school. They're on the phone. They said it's an emergency."

He brings the phone in, hands me the receiver in the dark. I roll over on the bed and hold the phone up to my ear.

"Hello."

"Hello, it's Rebecca Mintz. I have to tell you something."

"Is Augusta okay?"

"Yes, Augusta's okay."

"Did she run away?"

"No, she's fine. She's here."

So now what? Tell me.

"We have had a difficult situation here," Rebecca goes on. "We're dealing with it. Aaron Golden has committed suicide. We just found his body this afternoon."

I don't care. My daughter is okay. My daughter is safe.

They were hardly friends, Rebecca tells me. He broke up with his girlfriend and then he disappeared and later they found his body hanging from a tree in the woods near the school. They are calling all the parents. All the kids are in a giant all-school group. Everyone is upset. But Augusta is all right.

I know this is a terrible thing. This is the worst thing that could happen to those other parents, but this is how you think when you get this way with your kid—that's all there is. All you care about is that your kid is all right. Everything else falls away. Everything else is burned away. There was a suicide and it is very sad of course but it is not my suicide and it is not my kid.

That's how it is. You know it's selfish, but you are unashamed of your desire for only your daughter. And you are unashamed of your uncaring. It doesn't matter. This one time your kid's okay. It's somebody else's.

We talk some more and she tells me Augusta will call me tomorrow and then we hang up.

Is Jack still awake?

I call into his room.

"Honey?"

He hardly answers me. And then I realize I haven't told him. "Augusta's okay," I tell him.

"You mean she's not dead?" he asks.

And I realize he has been waiting in his room, not knowing, waiting in the dark not knowing, scared for his sister in his room.

And I flash back to my son years and years ago lying in his

bed sad, worried, he was such a worried boy! Unable to sleep lying in his bed when I used to come up the stairs and peer down the hall, long after he had gone to bed, long after he should have been asleep, and there he would be, lying on his side, facing the door, and I could see his eyes shining in the dark, watching out into the hall, waiting because he couldn't sleep but he didn't want to get in trouble, didn't want to call for me again.

"Yes, she's fine," I tell him, and I go into his room and I tell him about the other kid but he doesn't care really either. Augusta's okay. That's what we care about. This time we're okay too.

✿

The day before we leave I sign the deal to sell the radio stations. I tell my people. Nobody is shocked. They all sort of knew anyway. Now there will come the bumbling-around part, everybody discussing it, looking at me weird. I'm glad I'm leaving.

We're all on the plane together—Ben, Jack, and I—and it's snowing hard and the plane's a nineteen-seater and icing up and they have to deice it and there's wind and it rocks through the stormy sky on the way to Rockland on the way to Boston and I think: What if we all go down? How would that be for Augusta? All her family.

She's not in good shape, they have warned me at the school.

✿

It's a long way west to Oregon, especially when you're traveling with a fifteen-year-old boy with no room for his legs. Es-

pecially when you're traveling with your ex-husband and going to see your daughter, whom you haven't seen in three
months and who, during that time, was missing for over a
week. It's a long way even by plane, especially when the
movie they show you is *Zorro* and all you have to read is old
magazines and a book you thought you'd like but really
don't.

We wind up late into Portland, missing the last plane out
to Bend, so we rent a car and drive, the three of us. There's
ice on the roads and our little car skids around. Ben drives
and Jack sits up front, and I lie down in the backseat, where
it's quiet.

It's dark out and my ex-husband is driving up and down the
mountains of Oregon. I can feel the little car climb the
windy roads. Up front I can hear them talking about cars
and boats and other things, things that don't interest me too
much. And I lie in the back, tired, curled under my down
jacket, with the seat belt off. I can see the edge of the sky
around the tops of their seats, and out the side window. A
couple of far stars and the black night. Lights ripple through
the car as trucks go by.

I can hear their voices talking quietly on and on about uninteresting things.

It feels like when I was a kid, riding in the backseat of my
parents' car with them in the front talking to each other. I
could hear their voices. I was tired. It was late. I could hear
them talking about things that didn't interest me, but the
sound of their voices was comforting. They sounded faraway. As if they were riding in another car, on another road,
somewhere else.

I'd be half asleep lying like this in the back.

I can see a piece of the sky. I can feel the car rumbling over the road. I can hear their voices and the silences between their sentences and I feel safe. Safe enough to sleep.

23

WHEN I WAKE UP we're at the Riverhouse. It's snowing and it's really cold. We drag our bags out of the rental car and check in. Jack and Ben go off to their room in another part of the hotel and I find mine right off the parking lot.

The room is the same as it was last fall, only now it's winter and more desolate. The bedspread, the drapes, the square plain television set all look familiar. The carpet, even. I set out my toothbrush in the little bathroom. Augusta will share this room with me for one of the nights I'm here. I got a room with a real fireplace that burns fake logs. We will have our Christmas stockings here. We'll be together.

Carefully I go through my little rituals so I can sleep. Put clothing in the drawers. My shoes in rows. I've always liked things in a certain order. Book by the bed. No glasses.

I left my glasses in Ben's rental car. I call his room. Jack answers.

He tells me Ben went out to get something to eat. He's not sure where.

So I put on my coat, my boots, and go out into the cold snowy Oregonian night. We're on a wide highway full of malls and restaurants. I am exhausted. Everything seems surreal. The bright lights of the passing cars. The snow coming down, the hard wind. It's really cold. I walk up the highway and cross dangerously and come to the first restaurant I find. He isn't there. The waitress looks at me with her blank eyes. I wonder how I look, in my Maine winter jacket, red faced from the cold, hood pulled up, exhausted eyes staring out.

I think the International House of Pancakes. That seems like him. I walk up on the snowy highway. This is not a place for walking, even in the day. At night it's crazy. Cars coming out, skidding around in the snow. It's late. The parking lots are nearly empty. I have to keep my head down, shoving into the hard wind, going forward, looking up in quick little looks through the snow to see where I am. There are bushes planted all around to define the various lots. I squeeze between their sharp little branches.

The International House of Pancakes seems fancier than I would expect. A certain lighting. Maybe just for Christmas. I push the heavy door open and stare into the room.

Everyone here is quiet and busy with their pancakes. I'm covered with snow.

I see a man sitting in a booth with his back to me. It's Ben. As I come upon him here, at night, sitting in the booth, waiting like any man would wait for his pancakes, here in Oregon, just before Christmas, as the snow falls down, he seems at once familiar and unfamiliar. Dear to me and completely foreign. We have known each other more than twenty years.

"I forgot my glasses in your car," I say, standing in my big coat by his booth.

He looks up, startled. He gives a little laugh. I always did amuse him. My odd ways.

"You walked here?" he asks me.

"I didn't have a car," I tell him.

He asks if I want to stay, but I don't want to stay. I just want my glasses. I want to go back to my room. He gives me the keys just as his pancakes arrive. There's a little tree on the counter with all lights on it. I get my glasses. They're right on the seat in back, just where I left them. I bring him back his keys and go back to the Riverhouse. This time the wind is behind me pushing me along, so it doesn't seem as far.

Another parent seminar. Now we're the veterans, and most of the other parents look familiar. I find Roz and Arnold and sit near them. My little buddy Alex from September's here. We are impatient with the introductions; this time we know which ones are never going to shut up. Which ones will cry. We listen to the official explanation of the suicide. They talk about grief counselors, special groups, dealing with it. There will be a special session later for those interested. Two psychologists from Bend will speak to us about teen suicide, and about the effect of this suicide on our children.

I want to get Rose alone and ask her about Augusta. All the parents want to get her alone to ask about their kid. At the end of the lower school session I manage to be face-to-face with her.

"Oh yeah," Rose tells me. "Kid's got some problems. I'm worried about her. They did some tests on her. She's border-line. Definitely."

Then she can't really talk to me because of all the other

parents wanting to know about their kids. And so I'm left with this odd, confusing proclamation. Borderline. I still don't even know what it means. Does it mean crazy?

"We're worried about her," they keep telling me, different counselors, some that look familiar, some that don't.

"Oh you're the one whose daughter ran away," one mother says to me in the ladies' room. Her son is graduating. She's wearing special clothes.

I answer stiffly, washing my hands at the sink.

"Are you okay?" she asks me.

"No," I say.

During the break I go for a cold walk. Do these people know what they're talking about? Are they just making everything up? The sky's a hard blue and there's snow everywhere. It's different from our snow, this West Coast snow. I take the walk I took last summer, and follow the river all the way into Bend, walking on that hard white snow. I am wearing tons of clothing. It's so cold.

At the special suicide session, everybody's there, sitting in a huge circle around the room. The psychologists, a married couple, are soft-spoken. Kind. Hip. Gentle. They're from Bend. They speak about suicide. Teen suicide. And while one is talking the other one listens attentively. They are very polite. When they're not talking, they sit quietly with their hands in their laps. Augusta has been seeing the lady. She told me she just goes to get out of class.

They talk about why children kill themselves. We get to ask questions. How to help our children deal with Aaron's suicide. How to know if our kid might try it, too.

I raise my hand and ask what if your kid has already tried

it? When I say my daughter's name, the woman psychologist looks at me suddenly alert, although her face is kind. She says that those who have tried it once do tend to be the ones who try it again. She says she would like to talk to me later, in private.

Her name is Sylvia. She is lovely; very thin and wearing beautiful green clothes. I could be friends with her in another place, but I do not expect to be friends with her here. Maybe she is the magician who will fix my daughter.

Ben and I sit down with her on folding chairs. It's all reminiscent. Everywhere it's the same—folding metal chairs, Kleenex, worried parents, us. This is the world we now inhabit. It's our classroom, it turns out. It's where we belong.

Sylvia tells us she is "concerned" about Augusta. That she has given her some psychological tests. I tell her what Rose said to me. Sylvia slightly wrinkles her perfect forehead.

"That's simplistic," she says. "I don't want to alarm you. But Augusta does demonstrate some borderline characteristics."

"Does that mean she's crazy?" I ask bluntly.

I want something here. Some measure. Something to go back with. Something I can hold in my two hands, turn around, get a sense of.

"No," she says. "It doesn't mean that."

She tells me what I've heard so many times before. That it is impossible to diagnose a teenager. That they're all a little crazy and that you can't make a definitive diagnosis based on one test, or even a series of tests.

So that's good.

They've got me going here. I'm up, I'm down. I don't know where I am. If she's crazy or if I am. I think about how I've been at various times in my life. A snapshot of myself at any given moment could seem to be a snapshot of a crazy person. I know one photograph in particular. Taken in a field outside London, 1970. I was stoned on acid. My torn blue dress, hair in a whizzle, staring eyes, my wild grin. I remember that I couldn't talk. Later, anyway, he let me drive. At that one moment, you could say I was nuts. But, taken overall, I guess I pass.

I tell Sylvia I don't think Augusta gets enough exercise, that she needs to be outside more. She agrees with me. She says she'll lobby for it. She doesn't think any of the kids do. She thinks Augusta ought to have more art. She writes these things down seriously on a piece of paper. Augusta. Art. Augusta. Exercise.

Ben says Augusta loves to see the ocean. That when she lived in Maine she always loved to go and look at the ocean.

So Sylvia writes that down in her little pad, too.

Augusta. Ocean.

I feel safer now.

But I'm exhausted. Clinton was impeached today. My daughter's crazy. She's not crazy. She might be crazy. Maybe with the art lessons. Maybe the ocean. I'm thinking I should come here. Not during parent seminar with all the other sad, bewildered cattle. On my own. Take her out to see the Pacific Ocean.

I imagine the two of us in a rental car driving across the flat wide area of middle Oregon. Out over the pointy Western mountains. Off toward the wide Western sea. We would stay in hotels and we'd watch movies on our hotel television sets and we'd talk.

But now I'm just tired out by the day. By all the emotion and the parents and the explanations.

I go into Bend and meet Roz and Arnold and their younger son, who's happy and regular and hungry. We all are hungry and we all eat big dinners and tell jokes. I know lots of jokes. Arnold knows lots of jokes. The boy knows jokes. And we tell those jokes one right after another, and we don't have to talk about our daughters at all.

In the morning I sit in my hotel room at the Riverhouse and drink coffee and think about the sale of the radio stations. I am going to redesign my whole life, at least on paper. I make lists of what I want to do. I try to imagine what it will be like not to work for a while. Hike whenever I want to. See friends. Go out. Write novels. I haven't taken more than two weeks vacation a year in twelve years. I have never taken more than one week off at a time. I don't know what I like anymore. I don't know what I want to do. When I was thinking about selling the stations I was afraid of this. It felt like a big abyss. Not having my job. But now it feels sort of wonderful. As if everything up until now has been decided but now nothing is decided. Now I get to choose.

We drive over to the school. There are lots of people there, parents and graduates and other students all milling around. I recognize most of the kids now.

We go over to Augusta's cabin and when she sees Jack she screams she's so excited.

She shows him her room. He stands there awkwardly. There are four other girls there, all looking at him. Augusta's brother.

She parades him over to the main building. The graduation is in fifteen minutes. Everybody is chattering and excited. Ben and I stumble along behind our two children. I want to touch them. I just want to see them together. To see how they love each other. They've never been apart this long.

The graduation ceremony is held in the gym. It's big with all new wood and huge windows. The sun pours in. It's really hot in the metal folding chairs. The ceremony takes forever even though there are only the four graduates.

Afterward there's a buffet lunch in the dining room and lots of fizzy fruit punch and lots of food and people stuffed in there with paper plates and congratulations. I just stand there, stupid with the heat and the noise. All I want to do is look at my two kids, my tall son and my beautiful daughter in her special graduation skirt ("Look at my skirt! Look at my new shoes!"). All I want to do is to see them walking around through the milling crowd together arm in arm, Jack a little embarrassed, so tall and cute, and Augusta holding his arm telling everybody: *This is my brother. Look! this is my brother. Doesn't he look like me?*

Her hair is shorter. She seems younger. Later, in the car, driving into Lyle, with all four of us crowded into a car together, she says she wants to go swimming at the Best Western. She wants dinner with Becca and Roz and Arnold and Becca's little brother at Pizza Hut. She wants to go to the big drugstore. We all walk around in the enormous drugstore, her father and I lurking behind, watching in case she steals something, in case she tries to run away.

Later, in the car, I give her two Christmas presents—the book and the fuzzy blue sweater. She tears them open, grabs up the sweater. "I love it, Mommy!"

She seems so young. We go back to the Best Western, where we're meeting Roz and Arnold, and we sit in their enormous chairs and we chat, Roz and I, Becca and Augusta, and it could be normal, almost, but of course it's not.

✿

The next day is the day we have our meetings with Rose.
This is the one where Augusta tells us what we did wrong.
Last time she had to tell us everything she'd done. Now it's
our turn. I'm first.

Rose and Augusta and I sit knee to knee in Rose's office.
Augusta takes out her paper. She has written down all the
things I did wrong.

She says I never seemed like a mother to her. I seemed
like a bad roommate.

She says I yelled at her.

She says I wasn't ever there when she needed me to be
there.

She says I wouldn't let her do what she wanted to do.

She says I tried to control her.

She says I never listened to her.

She says it never seemed as if I loved her.

She says I kicked her out.

She says I sent her away.

She says I never tell the truth.

Her mouth has this little crimp in it as she says these
things. She reads these things calmly, almost matter-of-
factly, but I know that sad crimp. What it means. That this is
very hard.

Then it's my turn. I don't know what to say to her. I say, "I
always loved you. I always loved you and Jack. But it was
hard. Your father and I had a terrible marriage. He's a good
person. We just couldn't be married to one another. And
when we got divorced I had to go to work for my mother.
Can you imagine that? I didn't want to. I wanted to write
stories. But I had to. I had to support you. And it was horrible. I was so scared. I didn't know what I was doing. I didn't

have any money. Everybody at the station resented me. I was the boss's daughter. I felt like a failure, going over there. Working for my mother. I didn't know anything about the business at first. And I didn't know how to raise you. I had to make it up. I was so scared. I was scared all the time. It was so hard. The house. The two of you. The job. But I loved you, and we did have some good times, didn't we?"

I look at her with my eyes full of tears and she looks back at me and she has a different look now. Maybe she can see me. It's such small steps.

We hug each other and I give Rose the present I got her at the Grasshopper Shop—a deep red scarf knit of chenille. She likes it right away and puts it on over her big sweater.

I get to talk to her alone awhile.

I am stunned by everything Augusta has said. She's right, I think dumbly. I tell Rose, "She's right. I wasn't any good. I did things wrong."

Rose tells me it was fine what I said.

And I hug her, too. I think, after all, she is wise.

We get Augusta for a whole day and overnight. The kids and I drive into Bend. We wander through one of the malls together. Augusta gets her hair cut. Jack plays video games. It feels unreal. Everywhere we go we see her friends from the school walking with their parents through the mall.

We wind up eating lunch in a hippie place downtown, the three of us. It seems familiar and unfamiliar being together. They make fun of my soup, of my big coat, of my haircut. We go back to our room and have room service and watch TV. I am trying to think this is ordinary, I'm trying to enjoy this time with my children, but it all feels weird.

Later, while the kids are with Ben, I finish wrapping their stocking presents. I have already given Augusta the sweater and the book. She still loves presents. I would do anything, I would give her anything, just to hear her say it again— Mommy, I love it!—the way she said it when she saw the fuzzy sweater.

❧

Morning in our hotel room. I wake up first and Augusta is sleeping in the other bed. It's so quiet. She sleeps the way she has always slept—as if someone has thrown her into the bed. Hurled her there. When she wakes, she looks around completely bewildered.

Jack comes in in a little while. They want the stocking presents. Augusta lights one of the fake logs in the fireplace and we have a fire and try to pretend it's cozy and not weird. And it actually is cozy—the three of us together again, performing this odd adaptation of our Christmas ritual. Mommy on the bed. Children grabbing down their stockings. Everybody taking turns.

I have given them silly little presents as if they were still young. Crayons that smell like different things: lumber, oranges, roses, dirt. Candy. Yo-yos. New Scotch tapes.

We have breakfast together in the hotel dining room. I sit at the table with both my kids and it's like a dream.

Then we drive back to the school for one last summation with Rose, when we talk about this visit and about my next visit, in February. Ben will stay on for a few more days now. I take pictures of my children together outside in the snow by the different buildings of the school. I want to get the snow in, show the sky. Show how beautiful it is out here. I want to get both my children into the pictures. I want their two faces.

I want their legs. I want all of them in the picture together. "Stand like that," I tell them. "Get closer together."

On the drive back to the airport at Dalton, Jack and I are quiet. I take him for lunch to Shari's, where I ate last summer. I look in vain for my tall waitress. I don't see her. Maybe she's on another shift. Maybe she doesn't work here anymore.

I decide, sitting there in the quiet booth, that Augusta will be all right. That she will come back. That the tests, the things they say might be wrong with her, aren't true. I know she'll be fine. I could tell by the way she held her brother's arm, the way she liked the sweater, the way she talked to me in Rose's office. She's going to be okay. Maybe in the summer she can come home. Maybe next fall.

Meanwhile I'll come back alone and visit her. We've planned on that. I'll take her somewhere. It will be a special time. I can do this now. I don't have the stations. I can go anywhere I want. And she said she'd like to.

All the way home, flying across America, I am thinking of my daughter at the school. It's two days before Christmas. The airports are clogged with people. Every single flight is delayed. We are stranded in Las Vegas in the middle of the night for five hours dozing on black chairs waiting for our plane. I fall asleep and wake again and look at the crowd belching out of the gates. The people of Las Vegas with their hard yellow hair and their tanned faces and their fancy glittery clothes. Around 1 A.M. a crowd gets off a flight from L.A. Everybody is greeting everybody else and then, last of all, the glum-faced stewardesses with their neat navy blue suits, pulling their navy blue suitcases on little wheels. There are four of them. They look exhausted, but ridiculously atop their heads are red felt antlers. Maybe they forgot they had them on.

24

WHEN I GET HOME the stations are sold and it's time for Christmas. My sister is coming up with her family. We'll all be together at my parents' house, all except Augusta. There's a lot to do. I am excited about seeing my nephews. They are young and easy and fun to be around. Then it will be New Year's Eve and I don't have to work! For the last ten years I have always had to work at the WWMJ New Year's Eve Oldies Dance Party, bundled in a big coat in the lobby of the Ellsworth Holiday Inn. People would come in with a blast of cold air and I'd smile. "Happy New Year!" Later there'd be the limbo contest and party hats and plastic goblets of champagne and "Pretty Woman" blaring out and "I Heard It Through the Grapevine," and I'd catch my boyfriend's eye in a rueful glance.

And then it would be midnight and the bright new year and the place would be full of smoke and popularity and noise and Fred Miller would yell into the mike and the crowd would yell back and we'd all hug one another and bump our paper hats together and there'd be noisemakers honking and people shouting and it had begun: another year. Another great big year.

And later, tired, stinking of smoke and spilled champagne, we'd drive home through the cold night on the dark road, streetlights blinking aimlessly, as the snow began.

Only this year I no longer run the radio stations. This year my boyfriend and I will have a quiet dinner at Redfield's in Northeast Harbor eating fancy foods and having glasses of perfect wine. We won't talk much about the year that's over. It's finally done, that's what counts.

I think it was the worst year of my life. But it has ended all right. And here we are—we're still together. And Augusta thank god thank god will be all right. And Jack's all right. The new year can begin.

On my birthday in early January she calls me. "Mommy!" she says. "Happy Birthday!" She sounds terrific.

"I can't wait to see you!" she tells me. "I can't wait. Twenty-two more days."

I am going out in February.

"Happy Birthday, Mommy. I can't wait."

✥

It's the end of January. It's the cold bone of winter. It hasn't snowed much yet, so I'm still hiking. One day I go up Cadillac. I can't believe it. In January. I go up from Blackwoods Campground, the long way. Up through the rooty dark woods, opening out onto the rocky slope. There's no one about. It's cold and the sky is a flat white gray. The ocean, the rocks, the sky, and the trees are all various shades of gray. There's little joy in hiking on this day. It feels hard and long and too cold and my sweat makes me clammy in my clothes, but I keep going. It's my promise to myself to climb the mountains. At the top the parking lot is abandoned. The little shop is closed. There are no buses. I stand and look out at the islands lying flat on the flat sea. The island where I used to live. The farther islands where I went one winter, twenty years ago, in a tiny plane on a cold cold January day. I feel chilly up there on the mountains in my clammy clothes, but when I start down I feel very strong. I go fast, leaping from rock to rock going down the southern side of Cadillac Mountain.

A few days later I climb Day. It's sunny and the woods are dappled. The moss looks green. The puddles in the path are frozen. Dark leaves are trapped in the ice flat out and perfectly preserved. There's no one here, either, though the trail is easier and it's more likely that I'll meet someone hiking here, so close to Seal Harbor.

The sun feels great at the top and I go down the long way on the carriage roads. As I'm walking the road curves around before me all the way down. The sun is shining on the sea all around. I see the curve of the road before me and while I don't know what's around the curve or what comes next, it's all sunny as far as I can see. And I think: This is what I will imagine. This is how I'll picture my life. The sunny curve of the road. The sea all around.

Then things start to happen. A boy gets killed in a car accident on Eagle Lake Road. Four of Augusta's friends suffer burns in a fire when the ice shack explodes where they were sleeping. One of them was arrested the night before. One of them might not live. They take him to the hospital in Portland. It's the end of January. And it's really cold.

It's the night of the blue moon.

I'm asleep. I don't hear the phone.

Jack gets it in his room. Comes into mine.

"It's the school."

Groggily, I pick up the telephone next to my bed.

"Augusta's missing. She took off with another girl. We've notified the police. We'll let you know if we get anything."

So that's it. She's gone again.

And this time I don't wait to tell Jack or my parents. My mother is slumped down with the news. My father is stern and busy with his chores. My sister is whipped back into action in New York, back on the phone, back to the Runaway Switchboard. Missing children. Homeless. All of it.

It all feels too terribly familiar.

I walk up Schoolhouse Ledge again. Think about her missing again. It starts to snow. I don't know what to do with myself. It could go on like this. She could be missing for a while. She learned things, last time, how to do it. She could keep hidden longer. We might have to wait a long time.

So I go to work. I've just started my new job as a professional fund-raiser. I put on my shoes and go to a meeting in Bangor. What else is there? But on the way up, driving there all dressed up in my work suit again, in my heeled shoes again, in my big coat against the cold, I start crying and I don't think I can stop. But I do stop. I stop cleanly, perfectly, in time for the meeting. Afterward I go back to the parking garage and I get in my car and I sit in the dimness of the garage and I put my head down on the steering wheel, feel the hard curve of the steering wheel against my forehead, and I start to cry again. I cry and I cry. And I cry later driving back from Bangor down the bright road. She's gone again. Augusta, gone.

🌀

On the fourth day she calls me at night. Jack and I are trying to eat supper. She's all right, she says. She had to figure out a way to call me so I couldn't trace her. She used the Runaway Switchboard. They'll call your parents for you, put you through so they can't trace your call. I don't care. I'm talking to my daughter. She's all right.

Jack gets on the phone upstairs.

"Are you okay?" I keep asking her.

"Where are you?" Jack asks, but she doesn't want to tell.

She promises to call the next day. She says when. She's all right.

I call everyone when we get off—Ben, my parents, my boyfriend, Roz, my friends, my sister. I call Rose.

I go to bed and I am happy. I think I'm too excited to sleep, but I sleep hard and deep and fully and wake up at exactly four forty-four and remember that I'm happy.

By the time she calls the next day I've already decided we're through with Forest Ridge. It isn't working. Not for us. It might work for some kids. But not for us. So. Now what? I don't know. But I know I'm not sending my daughter to a lockup. I'm not sending my daughter to a psychiatric hospital. I'm not sending my daughter to another big program in the West. She's coming home. I don't even have to think about it. We'll figure something out. At least I can talk to her now. She called me.

And besides, we've done all that stuff. We've tried all that. And maybe it was the right thing and maybe it wasn't. It was the thing we did. We didn't know what else to do, I tell her later. We didn't know. So we did that. And now we're doing something else. No more Rose. No more folding chairs. No more groups. She's coming home.

She calls again. They're staying with a Christian that she met.

"She's really nice," she tells me. "She's really nice to us. She buys us ice cream, even though she's poor, and lets us watch movies and she lets us smoke.

"We went to the mall near here," she tells me on the phone. "We tried on prom dresses. It was really fun."

She wants to come home. She tells me there's a deal for kids through the Runaway Switchboard. It's called Home Free and it's for kids who have run away and want to go home. They send them free by bus. She wants to come home by bus.

I want to send her a plane ticket and bring her back right away. I could see her in a few hours. But I know. I know it's better if she finds her own way back to us. If she comes home herself. And I know she wants to do this. She's always wanted to do everything herself.

"Okay," I tell her. "I'm so glad, Augusta."

"You're not going to send me back to the school?"

"No, we're done there."

"You're not going to send me to a lockup?"

"No."

"They said you're going to send me to a lockup."

"No, I'm not."

"I can come home?"

"Yes. You can come here. But there have to be some rules."

"What?"

I tell her over the phone. That she has to go to school or be working toward going to school. I tell her no drugs and no drinking while she's living here. I tell her no smoking in the house. I tell her she can smoke on the porch. I tell her that she has to tell me where she's going. That she has to be in by ten.

"Okay," she says. "Okay. I'm coming home."

"I can't wait," I tell her.

"I love you. I'm so glad," I say.

When we hang up the phone I look around the room at my quiet house. How it's been since she's been gone, just Jack and I. The books all in their shelves. The quiet couches.

I've been trying to come to terms with her being away, but now suddenly everything is different again because she's coming back.

I'm happy, of course, but it's also going to be hard. We have to figure out a new way because none of the old stuff worked. The rules. The lack of rules. Kicking her out of the house. Letting her go. Making her stay. Calling the police. Searching her room. Telling her to tell me. The private school she didn't get into. The alternative school she wouldn't get into. The hospital. The doctor. The shrink. The trip to Boston with her father. The Wilderness Program. The expensive emotional growth program. The other shrink. The visits. The meetings. The sessions. None of it worked, really worked.

There are plenty of programs to try. Programs that work for some kids. Programs that work for 50 percent of the kids who go through them. Programs that work for 40 percent of the kids that go through them. And what does "work" mean? And what exactly happens to the other 50 or 60 percent? The kids who don't come through it? And what happens to their parents? Do they give up? Do they finally say okay, they've had enough, and turn their backs on their children? Do they let them "hit rock bottom," let them get hurt? Let them come limping back later, chastened by life? Bored by being poor and broke and broken.

The question is, how broken do they get?

And then what?

The hospital?

Medication?

And when does it end? They either get well or they die. That's the bottom line. Or they don't get well and they don't die but they ruin their lives. They become drunks or drug addicts or just dull-eyed people working at Burger King and lucky to have that, living in lousy apartments, stuck in bad relationships with men who beat them up or just ignore them. They have babies or they don't have babies. They have abortions or they don't get pregnant. They get AIDS or they get something else. They smoke. They have a terrible cough. They cough over the phone. They call you from bus stations. They call you collect. They aren't heard of for months. Years. They are the people they used to be afraid of. They're the people you told them not to look at. They are in cities. They are in shelters. They are in doorways. They are in your house. They are yelling in the doorway and they are no longer cute and you can no longer take them in your lap and hold them and keep them safe. You cannot stop their crying, or love them anymore. You can't even love them now.

I have four days in which to prepare for her. I have to figure out what to do next.

25

THERE'S A SCHOOL in Camden for kids who have dropped out of school. I read about it years ago in the *Maine Times*. It's run by a guy who grew up around the corner from me in Washington. He was in my sister's class. I didn't know him then, but I recognized his name when I read about him all those years ago and I thought: How funny. And I liked the way the Community School looked—a bunch of hippie misfits. It looked familiar. Looked like Antioch. Like my past.

When I read about it then I had no idea that one day I would be calling there myself, looking for a place to put my daughter.

I called Ray last spring, when things were really getting bad. I described the situation, and he sent me some literature about the school. But you had to be sixteen and Augusta was only fifteen at the time, and also it was clear that to go there and to succeed there you had to really want to finish school. It's a tough program. The kids go there for six months. They live together—eight of them—four boys, four girls, all kids who haven't been able to make it in regular school, all kids who have had problems with their parents or maybe with the law or maybe just in getting through the dark jungle of adolescence. They have to get jobs and pay part of their board and they have to study at night and go on week-end camping trips, and do special projects and pass certain tests, and help with chores and cook the meals. They learn to mediate. They are required to get along with one another. And at the end of the six months if they've done all that they graduate. And they receive a high school diploma.

The school's been around for twenty-five years.

Last spring Augusta was too stoned, and too angry, and too wild to make it through that program. But now, I think, maybe she's different.

I call them up and speak to Ray, and plan to drive down the next day to meet with one of the staff.

Augusta will be home in a few days. She's coming Greyhound. I've wired her a little money so she can buy some food. But not too much. It could get stolen. She could take off again.

By phone I discuss the possibilities with my parents, and with Ben.

There aren't too many options. There's the Community School in Camden. There's a program for street kids in Boston, but the counselor tells me that the kids are pretty rough there, mostly older, mostly heavy drug users, that a kid like mine might not survive it. There are prep schools of course, but she won't do that. There's the Alternative School at the high school, where Jack is thriving, but it's full up, and I'm not sure, anyway, that it'd work for her.

She's way beyond that now. I don't know what will work,

but I want her to finish high school. I'll go see the Community School in Camden.

Then my mother announces that she wants to go with me.

My mother is terrible in her grief. Where I have tried to look upon this as a jaunt—a little drive to Camden on a cold sunny February day—she gets into the car like it's a hearse and sits beside me like a sack of rocks.

I play her the new radio station The Bay. Old swing tunes. "Isn't this great?" I ask her but she stares ahead.

This is all my fault.

The drive to Camden is usually a pleasant drive, but today it's a dead drive.

My mother in her weary seat beside me.

The brassy bright sky shining in the car.

At every curve the wide sea opens up beside us and I want to gasp aloud at the prettiness of it, but then I glance at my mother. She just sits there.

I remember this.

My mother's set face looks the way it did when I got kicked out of Madeira.

I will never forget the day we went back to see the Headmistress at the school. I was seventeen. My mother went to plead with her to let me graduate with all the other girls with their red roses. We sat in the office of the inscrutable Headmistress, the two of us banded together on a little couch. My mother was forceful, eloquent, persuasive, and warriorlike in her determination, but it didn't work. It was like talking to a stone lady at the stone desk before us. A big stone gray-faced lady.

"I'm sorry," the Headmistress told us finally, "but I would

be doing a disservice," I think she said, "to Martha, to the other girls.

"This is a serious infraction," I think she said.

And I, bored, furious, embarrassed, listened to her, tried to think what she meant by that—infraction? Algebra equation? Chalkboard? But in fact I was humbled by her hardness and her coldness. I felt, as she wanted me to feel, shamed.

Who knows if that shame was what turned me further? I was already pretty wild by that time, already taking acid, sneaking out at night, sleeping with my boyfriend. Hitchhiking through Washington at night.

But would I have, in other circumstances, turned back in?

This is how I imagine it: that I, and then my daughter, somehow got off the path, veered off somewhere and then went whacking through the forest by ourselves. Running through the forest, off into the woods. The branches scraping at our faces, mouths open, laughing, calling back, mouths open but no longer laughing, yelling, maybe, running out into the pathless wood.

I don't know how either of us found our way out.

But then I think my friend's right. There's no magic key.

I don't remember everything that happened, but I remember some things. And I remember this. Driving back with my mother from Madeira through the leafy glen of deep Virginia after that last cold interview in the Headmistress's office. I remember sitting beside my mother in the car. My mother just driving. Never speaking. Steering the VW through the roads of suburban Virginia back to Washington. Her face as stony as her face right now. Hands clenched on the steering wheel just the way her hands grip her pocketbook today. And I remember looking at her and seeing her start to cry. My mother, who so rarely cried, was crying as hard as she had ever cried in her life. My mother, who could do anything, who was six feet tall, who could do anything, could no longer drive. She pulled the car over and she sat there. She did not bow her head, did not get out and walk along the shoulder of the road, did not say anything. She just sat in the car and cried and cried and cried.

But she does not cry now. She sits beside me full of the stones of her tears. She sits beside me like a sack full of rocks. There is no conversation. Nothing will ever be right.

The school's in a white house on a regular street in Camden. There are some teenagers around—tall teenage boys with long hair and a girl with a nose ring and bright orange hair cut short, and they say hi to us but are not curious. Two women greet us as we come in, my mother with her pocket-book, me with my pad of paper for taking notes. I have been taking notes through all of this. It embarrasses my children. Mommy's notebook. But what else can I do? Taking notes all through the crises. Writing in my journal. Making lists. Copying down the lopsided circle and the spearing daggers of the world. Driving in the cartoon wedge to save my daughter. On the telephone I'm taking notes. "Secure facility," "holistic approach," "condition presents itself"—those catchy phrases once new but now familiar. What's the language here at C-School? I'll learn it!

Our staff person is friendly, smiling, with curly hair and blue jeans. She seems glad to see us.

"Oh hi! I'm Karen! I talked to you on the phone!"

She reminds me of my friend Marie. So cozy.

The kitchen is slapdash and familiar. Reminds me of shared houses in Ohio. Five of us on co-op in a farmhouse.

Masking tape on a jar in the refrigerator—*This is mine! Lay off!* Mismatched silverware and mugs with words on them. On the wall is a chart of the chores. Names of the kids who are here now. Will Augusta's name be written here? Will she be here? Will I be visiting and sure of myself in this rambling place? The narrow dining room with its long table. A man with a big white beard and bare feet. Shelves full of books. A messy little office. A girl bounds by me with a bright tattoo. A poster on the wall: *Gay? Need to talk?*

I glance at my mother. She's a stone.

We go into the living room. It looks like all the living rooms of co-op houses. Indian print thing on the couch. More books. A huge TV. Some chairs. A long low bench beside a window. Posters on the wall. Paintings by kids.

We three sit down and Karen closes the white door.

She tells us about the C-School. How it works. What the kids do.

I tell her, gingerly, about my daughter. Some of what has happened. Some of what she's done.

Karen doesn't seem fazed.

"It seems to work," she says about the program. "The kids who come here really want to do this. It's a big accomplishment. It's hard. But they do it. They really want that diploma and they're ready. They're treated with respect here. Regular schools don't work for lots of kids."

"They didn't work for me," I say.

She laughs. "Or me," she answers back.

My mother has remained silent. She sits in her suit in the big chair and looks around. The paperback books shoved into shelves. The curtains hung crazily at the windows. The big couch.

"Well, I've seen enough to know what I think."

She's roused from her stupor. She's the mother I know. Decisive, energetic, definite. This is going to be it. And Karen, even though she doesn't know my mother, knows it too. This is it. What my mother says *goes.*

We both look around at her expectantly like two bad kids ourselves.

"This *looks* like Augusta. She'll *love* it here. It's not my cup of tea"—here she shudders slightly, thinking, I know, of the sticky kitchen counters—"but it's *perfect* for Augusta. I have no doubt."

Augusta will have to get in. She'll have to come down for an interview. She'll have to do some tasks to get accepted. Earn her way. She'll have to prove to the school that she wants to do this. They take only eight kids for every six-month session. They want kids who are going to make it. The program is expensive. There are scholarships, but I'm not asking for a scholarship. I've sold the stations and I've got the money. I want her in. I don't want anything to get in the way of getting her in, unless it is herself.

On the drive back my mother is a little better. But she is like someone who has had a long fever. She is tired. She is quiet. She is frail.

On the way back the sun is shining and the ocean, on our right this time, is blue and sparkling—unusually beautiful on this bare winter day.

"I want to show you something," she tells me, and she directs me to drive up a fancy driveway to the new conference center that the credit card company MBNA has built outside of Camden.

"Are we allowed up here?" I ask her.

She shrugs.

"We'll just tell them we wanted to take a look," she says.

She's beginning to sound like herself.

The driveway is long and perfectly paved.

It curves up an enormous hill and emerges out of the trees onto a big wide open space with a panoramic view of everything.

The building itself is in its own way wonderful. Shingled, meant to fade and look like other old Maine cottages. There's the inevitable enormous naturalistic statue—an animal of some sort, a moose or bear. There's a wide porch reaching all around the side of the building, all with the wonderful view. We park the car and walk around on the porch and look in the big glass windows. I feel like a thief here.

"Come on!" my mother says. "Look at that table in the conference room," she directs me. "Look at those chairs!"

She loves this place. This is her kind of place.

"Look at what they've done," she tells me. "Just look at what they've done."

She would like me to like this place along with her. I sort of do. She has always wanted splendor for her children. She has always wanted the big success. The closest I've come— certain boards and honors—have pleased her. But she wants more. But what do I want?

We stand on the big porch of the big building looking out at the sea and it is beautiful. We have come away from the slapdash kitchen of the Community School. Come away from my own scabby yard. Come away to this new vision of what Maine can look like.

"Isn't this beautiful?" she asks me.

❀

The next few days are busy as I get ready for my girl's return. Over the phone I've told her about the C-School. She thinks it sounds all right.

"But what if I don't get in?" she asks me already.

"Then we'll go to Plan B," I tell her on the phone.

"What's Plan B?" she asks me.

"We don't have one yet," I say. And she actually laughs.

I have a lot to do to get ready. I have to fix up her room. New sheets. Some flowers.

She will arrive on Thursday.

Ben and I both plan to go and meet her.

She will come into Bangor. On the bus.

On the way up I stop and buy a bouquet of yellow roses for my daughter, and lay them carefully on the seat beside me.

I'm excited and nervous and happy. My girl.

At the Bangor bus station I wait for her. Groups of people come through the station but she doesn't come. Two teenage girls with body art and tight jeans carrying backpacks come through, look scornfully at everyone who's waiting there, but they're not her. A man with a nervous tic comes in, sits down, and handles his red beard with nervous fingers, gets up, comes back, sits down, picks up his newspaper, and puts it down. A young woman with long hair comes in. She has a little daughter with pink sweatpants and pink bow barrettes in her thin, shiny hair. The daughter looks around at me. The mother sits down, puts the little girl into her lap. She has a book to look at with her daughter.

I have a book myself to read, but I can't read it. I open it up and look at the pages but I can't read the words. I don't know what they're talking about in this book; talking about things that happened, things that didn't happen. I don't care.

I have the roses on the plastic seat beside me. Hidden in green paper. They're okay.

It's been too long. There's something wrong.

I go to the desk.

"The bus from Boston?"

"Oh, that one came in twenty minutes ago," he tells me.

Oh my God.

I go out quickly, out the back. There are big buses everywhere. And cars parked, and it is confusing. I have my purse in one hand with my book stuffed in, the roses in their paper. It's not cold. The sun's so bright. I look around the parking lot and then I hear her.

"Mom!"

She is with Ben. They're waiting by his car.

"Mom! Where were you?"

I go across to her, across the parking lot.

I whisper, "I was waiting."

I can't talk.

Later we all have lunch upstairs at Epi's. The sun comes in. We three sit together. Ben and I can't eat. Augusta's ravenous. We stare at her like we're the hungry ones. Her pretty face. Her newly dyed black hair. Her jewelry. Her blue blue eyes. She is exquisite. She's our daughter. She is back.

She's hungry and excited and full of her adventures on the bus. She jokes to us about the people that she met. Her new best friends. Her friends in Oregon. She wants to go back west. She wants to get her diploma. She wants to live in California, where there's sky. She wants to tell us everything. She wants to go home. She wants to see her brother. See her friends. See all her stuff. The ocean. Go on her special walks. She wants everything. She wants it all. Right now.

We stare at her. We're starving for her. Her wonderful vitality. Her charm. Her impossible, enraging, engaging, infuriating self. Our daughter.

We drive back in a procession to the Island. She rides with Ben. It's only fair. It's me she'll live with. I am the one who'll get to see her in the morning with her hair askew, or in the evening reading in a chair. I wonder how the house would look to me if I were coming home after so long. How did my own house look in Washington when I came home after I was gone so long? I remember it looked smaller. Familiar and unfamiliar. It looked different and it looked the same. How will our house look to my daughter now that she's back?

I don't know what to expect. I don't know what will happen. I wonder if we'll have a few good days and then right away be back at war. I wonder if she'll even stay here, or if she'll run away again. If she'll make everybody crazy. If she'll start doing drugs. If she's already doing drugs. If she'll be mean, or kind.

I don't know if she'll get into the Community School. If she'll even go there. And if she does, if she'll obey the rules. I don't know if she'll start right up with all her creepy old friends. If she'll start sneaking out at night again. I can see her little head in Ben's car as we drive homeward. I can tell she's talking about something in her animated way. I want to enjoy this, to just relax and concentrate on her return, not think about what's going to happen next.

❧

She surprises me by spending the first few days at home. She seems to want to be in her house. In her room. Sorting out her clothes. Complaining about what's missing. Reading her old magazines. Listening to music.

She takes a walk with me around the town.

We rent a movie.

She calls one friend, she calls another friend, but she wants to be home.

She gets a job a few hours a day helping my friend Susan with her business.

I take her over to Bar Harbor one day for lunch at Café This Way with Bea and the baby. The baby slumps in the seat and smiles at us. Augusta wants him to call her Aunt Augusta but he can't talk yet.

I don't know what language we're speaking in this odd silent sphere. I don't know what color anything is. This is like a little pool where we are together. It is undefined. She is here. How amazing, she's returned to me. We are in a delicate negotiation of sorts—trying to figure out what is best for her, my now black-haired girl with the blue eyes and the kind smile and the weariness and the experience and the faint scars on the inside of one wrist.

We are kind to each other. We are delicate.

She lets me hug her sometimes.

She lets me talk to her.

She will sit with me at the table.

She goes through the rooms of the house as I would have gone through the rooms of my house, the house I grew up in, if I had been gone for so long. She tastes the cookies and she touches the necklaces strewn out on my bureau. She goes into her room sometimes and stays there for a long time trying on her clothes, listening to music, reading old books she read when she was younger.

She does not want to stay here. This is temporary, and we both know that, so we forgive each other little things. I don't say anything about the cereal bowl she left on the bookshelf. She doesn't mention my noisy tread at 6 A.M. up and down the stairs of the house when I am on my way to walk up Schoolhouse Ledge.

We are in a temporary situation. An odd twilight.

Jack is subdued. He wants her to go everywhere with him. To make what she calls a "cameo" at the school, to go to the basketball tournament game in Bangor (which she would have always disdained, disdains even more now, after all her mad adventures). He is happy to have her here but she also drives him crazy.

I hear them at night in each other's rooms, talking away. They are best friends.

Her friends find out she's back and call and call and call. Boys with smoky voices who worry me. Girls with stupid names.

She treats me kindly, like an old dog. I know I am now dear and familiar and outgrown.

She has let go of me and I am learning how I will let go of her. I remember, when she was a baby, and I was still nursing her and suddenly pregnant again, with Jack, and I felt as if all the calcium were being sucked out of my bones, I asked the pediatrician how long I should nurse her.

"You have to give it up someday," he said. "That's what having children is all about—they're just on loan to you. You always have to give them up, first by giving birth to them, and then when you stop nursing them. Then they go off to school, then they leave. You're always giving them up."

I sort of get it now. She's who she is. I can tell her what I think, what worries me and what delights me, but I can't make her be a certain way. It has changed both of us, having her gone.

I tell her in the car that I hope she will use her tremendous talent.

She no longer hates me when I tell her she is wonderful. She herself knows she is wonderful. She understands that she ran away from the school *twice!* That she got herself home by bus all the way from Oregon with no money and no help really but the Runaway Switchboard.

She is proud and small and she tells me she wears makeup now, and she does wear makeup. She still smokes cigarettes but only outside and she puts the butts in a little can that she found for herself. We move through the rooms of our house as if we were characters in a play that involves dancing and careful choreography. The phone rings all the time. Someone is always in the bathroom. The children take turns driving the car. They are both practicing to get their licenses.

This is how it is now, at 17 Mosswood Road.

One minute ago I was carrying babies into the house. One minute ago, one crazy winter night, I was yelling *I can't handle this!* when one of them spilled their milk, and there wasn't any money, and my boyfriend had abandoned me. One minute ago I was pleading with the policeman to make her come home and now, any minute, she'll be gone and Jack will be grown up. Already he tells me that he won't be living here this summer, he'll be on the Island. He's got a job hauling traps with Danny.

Everything's different and keeps on being more different. The job is gone. The business sold.

We're hauling out the furniture and waiting for the checks to clear.

They took down all the trees behind our house. They've sold off one lot and someone has built a big new summer-house, truly ugly with bright shingles. They're going to sell off the other lot, which will probably mean another big summerhouse right behind mine, but for now, and until they do, from my windows I can still see the mountains through the trees. I can see the Sound.

epilogue

SEPTEMBER 17, 1999. It's the morning of my daughter's graduation from the Community School. We're all going. My parents are driving over from the Island. My sister and her family are coming from New York. Bill's bringing his wife and son and daughter. Ben, of course, and Jack. Augusta's friend Daisy. Bea might show up with the baby. And I'm going. I'm leaving in a little while to drive down. I have to do some work first, and I thought I'd climb Day Mountain. They say the hurricane won't reach us here. We've had some rain. It's probably all we're getting. The wind was wild last night, but it seems calmer now.

I have to get there early. I'm bringing her clothes. We bought her quite an outfit at the Bangor Mall.

My sister asked me to describe it.

"I don't want to give it away," I told her. "Just let me say two words to you: Leopard. Skin."

My daughter dresses the way I used to dress. She is sometimes the way I used to be. The way I guess I am. She even has a lot of my old stuff—the big amber ring from Copenhagen. The brown suede bag I got at the Sandal Shop when it was just a tiny factory on M Street in the sixties. She carries the same backpack I carried on the bus going to New Hampshire for Eugene McCarthy, heading out to San Francisco years ago.

She wants to go to California. That's her plan.

She's going to stay at home and work and earn some money. Then she's heading out.

On my desk before me I have the invitation to her graduation. She drew it. It's a drawing of a girl with wild hair and blue jeans and bare feet. The girl has big wings spreading out on either side and she is flying away from us out into a big sky littered with magical stars. In the distance there's a smiling, round-cheeked moon.

In Augusta's inimitable handwriting, she's written *Graduation Summer 99*, and this: *Shoot for the moon. Even if you miss it you'll still land among the stars.*

Every time I look at it it makes me cry.

Every time I think about her graduation, about what I might say during the open-mike part of her graduation, it makes me cry.

I told Jack that. He rolled his eyes.

"Why do you cry about it? Are you sad she's graduating? You should be happy."

"I am happy," I tell him, almost crying now, just trying to explain. "It's just emotional. I always cry about stuff like this. I cried when you graduated from kindergarten—remember, with that little cap they made you wear? I'll cry when you graduate from high school."

"Oh God," he says. "I'm not sitting with you."

I don't know what comes next. She's coming home for a while, and then she'll go again.

She's different now. She's younger and she's older all at the same time. She's lighter. I've seen it every time I've been down there to visit her, or when she's come home for a weekend. She's lighter.

I'm different, too. I guess I'm lighter, too. Without the radio stations. With a part-time job that has an end date—doesn't stretch disconsolately out into the future. *All my life I'll be doing this,* I'm no longer thinking. *All my life.*

With Augusta in Camden all this spring and summer and Jack on Islesford at his grandparents', I've had a chance to get to know myself again. To begin to figure out what I want to do with the second half of my life. In June, I went back to Madeira for the first time in thirty years and saw some of my old classmates at the first high school reunion I'd ever attended. Nobody remembered anything the same way. Nobody even remembered that I'd been kicked out. "You're kidding me. You mean you weren't there at graduation?" they asked me. "Are you sure?" Madeira no longer seemed terrible or even very big. It was dear to me now, and I realized, going back, in a way it was dear to me then.

Everything is different. In the next few years the children will be less dependent on me; and my parents, more. I feel as if time around me is at once enormous and frighteningly small.

But for right now the curved road ahead looks sunny. The kids are well. I'm working at something I enjoy. There is no crisis. Who knows how long we get this? But it's now.

I don't know what really helped bring Augusta through to this new, happier, lighter person that she is. The Community School was definitely great for her. But she couldn't have done it without everything else. I don't know if it was the

Wilderness or Forest Ridge or running away from Forest Ridge or coming home or the Carmelite nuns or my own steady perpetual prayer, or just time passing. Who knows?

We were all just thrashing through the woods in darkness. There was no map. We did what we had to do at every turn—took whatever path seemed to present itself. Thrashed through. Came here. And somehow we're all right.

But really it was Augusta who saved herself. That same proud, angry, powerful, loving spirit of hers that I used to battle with is the same spirit that shines through now.

Even during the worst of it, I knew that the very qualities that made me crazy during her adolescence would make her successful as an adult one day. If she could only stay alive that long.

It's a cold, rainy day in October. I worked all morning while the rain slashed down unevenly outside my window. This will bring some of the leaves down and another storm, later on, will bring the rest.

Early in the afternoon I drive over to Bar Harbor to eat lunch at the little restaurant where Augusta's working, saving her money to go to California. I drive her over every morning. She has to be at work at six. It's usually just getting light as we drive over through Seal Harbor, Otter Creek, past Jackson Lab. The roads are quiet and the sky is pink. Some mornings we are quiet, but sometimes we have wonderful conversations. She asks me things about my life. Old boyfriends. Jobs I had once. College. Sometimes she talks about things she's done. One time on the way over I asked her why she ran away from Forest Ridge. Why really.

"Five things," she told me. "I wanted to see a cat. I wanted to smoke cigarettes. To dye my hair. To go to a store. To have a boyfriend."

It was a year ago. The first time, when the call came that she'd run away. A year ago last night.

And now she is waiting tables in the Village Green Restaurant in Bar Harbor. She wears her little green shirt and her hair tucked back and all her rings. She smiles when she notices me sitting at my table. She brings my order over proudly, carrying the tray before her carefully in both hands, with the same proud, shy little smile on her face that I remember from the times when I would drop her off at school and she would be walking across the playground toward the door. The same look I remember on her face when she used to swim across the deep end at her swimming lessons, carrying her head up above the bright water, kicking the way she was taught to kick, scooping with her arms. And as I watched from the side of the pool in the humid air in mid-February I remember I could almost feel the water myself, its odd chemical thickness, almost feel my own self swimming as I watched her go.

acknowledgments

My thanks to Susan Taylor Chehak, Constance Hunting, Betsy Lerner, Denise Roy, and Liz Werby for helping me tell this story.